AF527878

Culture Change in India

Culture Change in India

Identity and Globalization

YOGENDRA SINGH

RAWAT PUBLICATIONS
Jaipur • New Delhi • Bangalore • Guwahati • Kolkata

ISBN 978-81-7033-555-9 (hardback)

Reprinted, 2025

© **Author 2000**

No part of this book may be reproduced or transmitted in any form or by any means, electronic or mechanical, including photocopying, recording or by any information storage and retrieval system, without permission in writing from the publishers.

Published by
Prem Rawat for **Rawat Publications**
Satyam Apts., Sector 3, Jawahar Nagar, Jaipur - 302 004 (India)
Phones: 0141 265 1748 / 265 7006
E-mail : info@rawatbooks.com
Website: rawatbooks.com

New Delhi Office
4858/24, Ansari Road, Daryaganj, New Delhi 110 002
Phone: 011-23263290

Also at *Bangalore, Guwahati* and *Kolkata*

Typeset by Rawat Computers, Jaipur
Printed at Nice Printing Press, New Delhi

Dedicated
to the memory of
LATE PROFESSOR A. R. DESAI

Contents

Acknowledgement

Most of the papers included in this volume were written during the 1990s. "The Significance of Culture in the Understanding of Social Change in Contemporary India" and "Sociology and the Emerging Challenge of Change" were delivered as my presidential addresses at the Indian Sociological Association's annual conferences held in 1992 at Delhi and in 1993 at Bhopal and both have been published in *Sociological Bulletin*. Similarly, "A Life-World of Disenchantment: Modernity, Ethnicity and Pluralism" was also published in the same journal; it is a lecture that I delivered in memory of the late Professor S. C. Dube at Jammu University in 1998. The paper, "Globalization and Local Cultures: Issues and Perspectives in India" was presented at the Biennial General Conference of the AASSREC, held at Beijing, China in October 1997, where as "Is Globalization a Threat to Regional and Local Identities" was written for a seminar organized by the K. Adaneur Foundation, held at Delhi in 1998. "Social Change: Rise of Popular Culture" was published in *India at Fifty*, edited by V.N.Naraynan and Jyoti Sabherwal, and published by the Sterling Publishers, Delhi in 1997. "Myth, History and Reason: Culture and Nation-Building in India" has been taken from the *Nation Building in India: Culture, Power and Society*, edited by Anand Kumar and published by the Radiant Publishers, Delhi in 1999. "The Desired Role of Political Leadership in Economic Reforms" was written for the Delhi Policy Group and presented at a seminar organized by them in 1998 at Delhi. Other papers too were written for seminars organized on related themes.

We thankfully acknowledge the contributions of the organizers of the seminars, publishers and editors who have helped in the preparation of these papers or for publishing them. Our thanks are also due to Rawats who have been a source of continual support during the publication of this volume.

Yogendra Singh
Centre for the Study of Social Systems
Jawaharlal Nehru University, New Delhi

Introduction

The process of change in the Indian society has entered a qualitatively new phase. Substantial material exists on the analysis of the changes in the social structure of the society, such as, its institution of social stratification and the processes of social mobility, the nature of demographic changes and the extent of urbanization and industrialization. The implications of the changes in power structure and the significant role that the emergent new power elite drawn from the backward classes are now playing in the polity, have been adequately examined. We have substantial material on changes in the caste structure and its functions, the profile of the community structure of the Indian society, its family systems and institutions of kinship and marriage. In the political domain, the process of nation-building and democracy, both in practice and at the level of ideology, have been thoroughly examined. The interface between economic development and the emergence of the new middle classes, both in the rural and urban centres, their role in modernization of society, specially in the fields of new professions, banking, management, media and information and many other sectors of services, etc., have drawn the attention of social scientists. Sociological literature in India has in a very substantial measure taken note of these changes in society.

The study of culture changes has, however, not drawn the attention of sociologists in the same measure as that of the changes in the social structure and its processes. This limitation in the sociological studies was noted by the Indian Sociological Association which deliberated on this problem at its annual session held in December 1992 at Delhi. The present volume of essays on *Culture Change in India: Identity and Globalization* is an effort to focus upon some of the significant processes of change in the domain of culture in India. To begin with, the first chapter, "The Significance of Culture in the Understanding of Social Change in Contemporary India" deals with various orientations in the work of Indian sociologists in their study of culture, the new challenges that such studies may now encounter due to the new processes of culture change through the emergence of the 'information society' and its consequences leading to the resurgence of the consciousness of identity among ethnic groups, minorities and weaker sections of society. It also refers to various facets of relationship between culture, its patterns and the processes of economic and political institution-building in the Indian society.

THEMES OF CULTURE CHANGE

The other essays in this volume focus primarily on the contemporary themes of culture changes in India. These changes could be divided into two categories: first, those which concern the substantive structures of culture and its relationship with social institutions; and secondly, those which refer to the processes of change in culture, specially engendered by the forces of globalization, telecommunication revolution and the emergence of market economy in a qualitatively new form. The structural issues of change refer to the impact of globalization upon local cultures in India (chapter 2), the nature of the cultural identities at the local, regional and national levels and the extent of their inner resilience to withstand the forces of globalization (chapter 3), and the emerging popular culture in India, its impact upon the style of life of the youth and other social categories in rural and urban population and the extent to which the western impact upon the changes in lifestyle threaten the cultural identity of persons exposed to popular culture (chapter 4).

A significant aspect, both of the rise in popular culture and the processes of globalization, is that these developments have direct bearing upon the nature of cultural identity and the dimension of the felt crisis. In case of the globalization process, comparative responses from the East Asian countries, such as Indonesia, Malaysia and Thailand, have been briefly brought into focus, particularly in the light of economic crisis these countries encountered following the flight of capital and the near collapse of their banking and market economies during the 1990s. These 'Asian Tigers' felt the acute fragility of economic and market globalization and its enormous social costs, and realize the need to be highly cautious in pursuit of their globalization policies in the fields of economy as well as culture. Comparatively, China remained unaffected despite its high rate of economic growth. We have examined as to how the elite in these nations views the advantages and limitations of the processes of globalization whether in the area of economy or culture. One may notice the cautious self-consciousness in China in comparison to the acute anxiety and sense of remorse for their policies on globalization as pursued in the past in Malaysia, Indonesia and Thailand. Obviously, these experiences have significance for India in forging its own policies.

The other substantive issues, such as the process of nation-building (chapter 5), language as the marker of cultural identity (chapter 6), the desired role of political leadership in economic development (chapter 7), the relationship between modernity and ethnicity (chapter 8), the changes in community structures and its cultural implications (chapter 9), and the impact of changes in social structure upon leisure activities and its institutions in rural and urban India (chapter 10) have been examined in the context of their significance to culture changes, both institutional and ideological. Finally, we have analyzed the implications of the globalization of cultures and of the emerging global market economy upon the teaching and research in sociology. How far could the market driven impulses in the field of education be reconciled with the need for research and teaching in fundamental areas of knowledge which immediately may not have utilitarian value? Could we evolve a workable and meaningful balance between research and teaching in the basic scientific domains of sociology and the sociology courses that are primarily oriented to marketability and employment? This debate does not merely have significance for the emergent crisis of the paradigms of education ushered in by the forces of globalization; these also by implication serve as pointers to the basic changes in the value system of the people based on the ideology of narrow utilitarianism. It has obviously wider and deeper significance for culture change at many other levels of its manifestation.

We have discussed the changes in culture in the context of the factors which are social, psychological and ideological in nature, and also influence the formation and crystallization of cultural identities. In this context, the phenomenon of cultural and symbolic domination of one cultural system over the other, occupies a very significant sociological space, deserving investigation. We have analyzed it with reference to the policy of the state about the Urdu language and its relationship with the Muslim cultural identity in India (chapter 6) and their institutional responses to meet with this problem. The processes of cultural conflict and the feelings of cultural domination, the movements for seeking legitimacy for one's own cultural practices or tensions involved in the processes of adaptation to new cultural traits etc., are not confined to the inter-societal or the international domains. Such conflicts also occur within a society among the local, regional and ethnic levels of culture.

Globalization expands the scope and speed of cultural interactions across societal boundaries; the incidence of migration and emergence of the cultural diaspora bring about intense cultural, social and economic interactions. This is made possible due to the telecommunication revolution but the cultural processes that it sets into motion acquire significance, related as these are to the possibilities of cultural assimilation, adaptation, integration or conflict in course of such cultural contacts.

To what extent does cultural globalization pose a threat to the cultural identity at the local, regional and national levels? What are the dimensions of social conflict and resurgence of identity consciousness that this process engenders? To what extent do the historical and the initial social-cultural conditions of a society provide resilience and dynamism to the local, regional and national cultures to meet with such challenges? We have maintained that in order to obtain a more objective and fuller perspective on these issues it is essential to keep in mind our initial historical and social structural conditions, which, to our mind, continue to influence the direction and shape of our cultural responses, whether it is in favour of adaptation to or rejections of alien traits of culture. From another perspective, which is meta-theoretical, it is held that each cultural system tends to integrate culture traits into a configuration which is guided by its core values; these values impose a logic of selectivity which define the limits of acceptance or rejection of alien cultural traits. Similarly, these core values within each cultural system also exercise the power of introducing adaptive changes in the meaning and usages of culture traits drawn from outside, and defines the modality and scope of its assimilation, integration or adaptation within the indigenous cultural system. Hence, the specific features of our social structure, its linkages with the local, regional, ethnic and national levels of culture and the core cultural values within each, should provide us insights into the contemporary forms of cultural changes.

Our traditional social structure enjoyed a great deal of the inter-structural autonomy. It could be seen to have existed among some key elements of the social and cultural systems. For instance, traditionally, there existed substantial autonomy among the principles of social stratification based on caste, the political system governed by the rulers and the value system and religious traditions which were under the control of the priests and local communities. The priests enjoyed cultural authority which was independent of the rulars. They had, and even now, continue to enjoy freedom to pronounce upon matters related to rituals, customary rites and ceremonies. Of course, local communities could also play some role in certain aspects of the religico-cultural matters based on tradition and local customs. Similarly, caste system enjoyed a large measure of autonomy through its panchayats and exercised self-rule in economic, social and cultural matters in day-to-day life. With the advent of the British rule, the state, for the first time began to encroach upon the traditional functions and rights of these institutions. Following independence in 1947, this process gained added momentum. It was implicit in the agenda of economic, political and cultural reform and modernization of the Indian society. Nevertheless, the role of caste, kinship and customary cultural practices where the priest presides has not been eroded. The recent studies indicate that caste despite major changes in its traditional occupational affiliation (which was hereditary in the past), has assumed new economic and political functions.

The social structure of caste pervades across religious and ethnic divides in our country. In the context of globalization and its impact upon our culture, the decentralizing and self-differntiating features of the caste system maintains, on the one hand, social and cultural pluralism and, on the other, also provides the capacity to the social structure to forge organic alliances or associations with other castes, communities or ethnic groups. It is already reflected in the country's voting patterns and upon its polity leading to democracy based on alliances with regional parties. These regional parties themselves mirror the impulses and aspirations of castes, communities and ethnic groups. An interesting feature of this change is that in the realm of culture, these local and regional social entities have shown capacity for selective adaptation to and integration of new cultural values and practices. Instead of being hurdles to the processes of cultural and economic modernization they have shown extraordinary degree of cultural and social resilience for adaptive transformations. It should not, however, imply that encounter with the global culture and economy is without conflict or resistance. The selectivity of their cultural responses is based upon a principle which discriminates between those traits of culture or economy which are perceived to be acceptable and, therefore, are adopted, and those which are seen to threaten identity of culture or tradition and are resisted. We witness a substantial measure of uniformity in terms of policy and normative or ideological evaluation in regard to the challenge of globalization, whether we refer to the nation, region or locality.

This helps us in understanding the relationship between local culture and its regional and national forms. A prominent sociological feature of the cultural tradition and social structure of India is that because of the pervasiveness of the caste system the local or regional cultures did not have an exclusive or segemetary feature as in many other societies. Each unit has, no doubt, its distinguishing cultural space and often contains unique traits and cultural practices, but at the same time each has maintained very vital organic linkage with cultural systems located at the regional or national-civilizational boundaries. With expanding number of the Indian Diaspora, now, these cultural linkages also extend to other countries and are tending to attain a global character. The revolution in modes of communication, travel, Internet, electronic-mail, e-commerce, fax and many other new modes of international and inter-cultural interactions have resulted, paradoxically, on the one hand, into the intensification of consciousness of identity, and on the other, selective appreciating and even adaptation to new cultural styles, forms and practices from other regions within India and from the countries outside India. On the basis of the pattern and direction of selective cultural adaptation that is taking place in India in the process of globalization of culture, and considering the historical features of its social structure and institutions, we have concluded that the Indian culture, whether local or national, has sufficient resilience to succeed in preserving its cultural identity and also work out a successful and creative synthesis between the global and the local, regional and national levels of cultural styles, forms and practices.

It is contended that globalization of culture also contributes to homogenization of its styles and practices. The evidence in this regard suggests that in several cultural fields a fusion of styles, contents and forms of culture is taking place. This is reflected in increased tendency towards creolization (amalgamation of words and phrases and linguistic usages) in languages, attempt towards fusion of styles in music, dance, painting, architecture and several other fields of culture. However, this process does not imply that the traditional or original forms and styles of cultural continuity and creativity cease to evolve. There is no replacement of the original forms with the experimental ones that attempts to fusion and harmonization bring into being. Instead of the original cultural styles and forms being eroded, these assume new meaning and significance since globalization not only brings several cultures and their institutions together but it also enkindles sharper consciousness of cultural identity.

The changes in traditional cultural practices and institutions are closely related to the processes of urbanization, patterns of migration, politicization of caste and community relationships in villages and the rapid pace of growth and expansion of the electronic media of information and entertainment throughout the country. These changes are also related to the transformation of economy. The abolition of the feudal system of tenancy and agrarian structure eventually contributed to the Green Revolution and increase in agricultural productivity. The peasants absorbed new technologies which altered the mode of production in agriculture and disturbed the equilibrium of many traditional cultural forms. Many traditional fairs, festivals, folk cultural celebrations, etc., which were linked with feudal patronage, had to undergo new institutional anchorage based on caste and community associations. In this process of transition, several cultural practices, organically linked with the past institutions, were lost. The traditional balance of relationship between the folk culture and the culture of elite, which have been extensively studied by social anthropologists, today stands deeply fractured at several places due to industrialization and urbanization and reform in many institutions of the traditional agrarian economy.

In addition to economic reforms, the processes of democratization and politicization of people and their social institutions have also brought about some major changes in the traditional culture. A significant consequence of politicization in India is the acute self-consciousness and celebration of identity by castes, ethnic groups and minorities etc. This change has broken down the traditional bonds of reciprocity and linkages of culture and economy among different castes and ethnic groups. Instead, each caste or ethnic group prefers to establish solidarity within its own fold, and seeks to achieve its social, economic and cultural objectives by constituting different associations and organizations. The breakdown in the traditional pattern of the inter-caste and inter-ethnic economic and cultural reciprocities has also been engendered by industrialization, expansion of education, the policy of positive discrimination in education, job opportunities and political offices, etc., in favour of the weaker sections based on caste and ethnicity. Consequently, a rapid change has taken place in the traditional occupational structure of castes and tribes. As these groups have moved to occupy new occupational space, many folk cultural traditions and forms that fostered inter-caste reciprocities have become redundant. In villages, the traditional community structure has been fractured as castes have been increasingly politicized. All these changes have affected the forms of leisure and recreation and brought about new problems of social and cultural alienation of communities both in the rural and urban society. We have discussed this problem and its processes in India in several essays contained in this volume.

CULTURE CHANGE AND THE ANALYTICAL CATEGORIES

The choice of analytical categories or concepts circumscribes the scope of thematic treatment of a problem. It also defines the premises and assumptions which underly the treatment of the cultural phenomena. The preference for a particular set of concepts for analysis of culture has also latent in its epistemological structure the choice of ideologies. On this basis, the value-neutrality of 'scientific categories' for analysis of phenomena has been widely challenged. In the opening essay in this volume, "The Significance of Culture in the Understanding of Social Change in Contemporary India", we have briefly discussed the shifting paradigms and choices in the uses of concepts for the study of culture and social change in India by sociologists and social anthropologists.

The overarching premise in our analysis of culture change is that despite manifestations of many new dimensions of culture change witnessed in the processes of globalization, the response to changes, ushered in by globalization remains within the discourse of modernity. This is so whether our frame of reference is the local, regional and national cultures, or we refer to the emergence of popular culture or the other levels of culture brought about by changes through revolution in telecommunication and mass media. This can be seen when we talk of democracy and nation-building, the desired form of political leadership for introduction of new economic reforms, or when we deal with community identities as reflected through rise in sensitivity for legitimation of culture as symbolized by language, customs, religious practices and style of life etc. The normative point of reference in most of these analytical studies of change is indeed drawn from points and counter-points within the ambit of the critique of modernity.

The focus on the pre-eminence of the role of rationality dominates most discourses on modernity. The analytical categories that we have used in this context (particularly in chapters 5 and 8), such as 'myth', 'history' and 'reason', are critical to our comprehensive analysis of this discourse. As widely accepted by sociologists, modernity implies a measure of 'disenchantment' from tradition. Tradition is supposed to be embedded in the 'enchantment' ideology about the life-world. Enchantment implies faith in the formulation that the normative principles governing life-ways in all of their aspects of manifestation have been 'revealed' by the Divine. It cherishes the faith that their origin is in the 'sources' that could not be challenged on the basis of utilitarian rationality as championed by science and technology. Historically, these are associated with the Enlightenment ideology. Even if we accept the Weberian explanation that in Europe the rise of rational capitalism, democracy and the social institutions based on rational legal authority owe their origin to the Protestant reforms introduced by Calvin, the fact remains that Weber also accepts that the nature of this rationality was governed by the reformation values which exhorted commitment to a moral order and personal ethic of conduct (anchored on the responsibility to the Divine according to that work was defined as 'calling', motivating the followers to perpetual self-less labour to make this world 'kingdom of God on earth') which gave rise to industrial capitalism. However, soon as the mantle of church was removed from this ethical foundation of rationality, the revolution of the industrial capitalism in Europe and elsewhere turned into an 'iron cage' bereft of moral sensibilities, being guided entirely by the profit motive and ruthlessness of the utilitarian goals.

The question, however, remains as to whether cultural sphere of our life, which outcrosses into the frontiers of economy, polity and social institutions, does indeed tend to be defined entirely by the utilitarian rational principles? Is there no scope in our rationalization or critical appreciation of our life-world and our social institutions for the application of normative or evaluative principles based on the supra-rational values? Also, to what extent does the history and collective memory of a people influence the manner in which they evaluate innovations in cultural, economic and social life? The contemporary discussions dealing with the discourse on modernity (including those which deal with economic, political and social-cultural globalization) increasingly recognize that the initial historical conditions as well as the universal and pervasive urge among people to legitimize their identity through celebration and re-invention of tradition enhances the significance of the supra-rational ways of defining normative issues. The role of myth and the mythic mode of normative legitimation is, therefore, continually revived and celebrated

The mythic sources for the search of identity and legitimation gain ground also because the scientific paradigm of rationality and utilitarianism fail to resolve several crucial problems of human condition which constitute the enigma of contemporary life in the 'modern' world. It is noticed that scientific reason not only explains but also mystifies reality. The solutions that science offers, on which the discourse of modernity largely rests, are not only revisable but often misleading. These have failed to resolve the issues which continue to bedevil the ideology of universal humanism and human rights. The asymmetries of power, exploitation of the weak by the strong, the continued social and cultural discriminations of people based on birth, gender, ethnicity, religion and nationality etc., have not ceased with the modernization of our life-world. These, and several other aspects of the contemporary processes of modernization, globalization and universalization of cultural and economic institutions, are, therefore, perceived by people not entirely through a 'scientific rational' prism. The scope for the mythic legitimation and rationalization of the cultural processes continues to enjoy validity in the ambience of ethical uncertainty and ambiguity which the contemporary processes of globalization of culture have generated.

The issues of cultural identity in the process of globalization, therefore, derive their legitimation from this complexity which is inherent in the rational utilitarian foundation of choices of values and life-goals in our contemporary life. It is imperative that we come to terms with this reality while analyzing the nature of culture change, as also the questions of new resurgence of the consciousness of cultural and social identities based on micro-situations, whether of locality, region or religion etc.; the process of cultural globalization and its myriad challenges should be observed and analyzed in the context of substantive and methodological problems which recognize this reality.

1

The Significance of Culture in the Understanding of Social Change in Contemporary India

Culture is a unique human reality. It emanates from the unity of humankind in nature, but it situates itself as a meta-natural reality. It is manifested in the technological, mental, moral, social, aesthetic and spiritual achievements of humankind. Culture gives meaning to our relationship with the other, as it also forms our subjective identity. Culture, therefore, enters into the processes of social change in many forms and at various levels. It defines the quality of social change as its indicator. By selective adaptations to outside cultural forces, it has a large measure of resilience. With all its institutional pervasiveness, it has a core which acts as a filter or a moderator to the outside forces of cultural contact and change. This also explains why in each mainstream culture one may find existence of sub-cultures and counter-cultures.

PARADIGM SHIFTS

Sociologists have been studying culture since the beginning of sociology in India, which roughly corresponds with the establishment of the British rule and the rise of the national movement. The trauma of the colonial experience inspired them to undertake critical appraisal of the indigenous cultural traditions, and it also made them conscious about the strong points of the western culture. The paradigm of cultural studies that evolved through this historicity led them to debate how the Indian tradition in its essential form could be made to adapt with the western culture without a loss of its core values or cultural identity. A deeper analysis of the textual culture, the cross-cultural comparisons of dominant traits and themes of culture, and a critical evaluation of the western constructions of the Indian culture and its evolution, were the main preoccupations of this period. This trend was reoriented to empirical-ethnographic studies of cultures. One set of studies contributed richly to the understanding of the tribal cultures, their intrinsic attributes and their linkages with other cultures such as those of the peasants, castes and regions. Yet another set of studies, largely under the influence of the American social anthropologists, focussed upon the phenomenon of culture in the context of the Indian community and its folk-tradition. A distinctive feature of this approach, however, was its sensitivity to the analysis of interactions between culture and civilization (Unnithan, Deva and Singh, 1965). The main indicator of the former as used, was the spoken language or the oral tradition, and of the latter, the written or the textual-elite tradition. Folk-elite dimension of culture was, however, not treated as a static continuum but as a historical reality embedded in the level of circulation.

The studies using this paradigm yielded rich insights into the structure and organization of the Indian cultural traditions. They also brought out in concrete terms the extent and direction of linkages that local cultures had with the cosmopolitan culture. The folk-elite and textual-contextual ties in cultural practices, beliefs and traditions were empirically mapped out. Community as a unit of cultural studies gave way to the concept of 'systems' which formed the basis of a new paradigm of cultural study through the notions of modernization. The focus of such studies shifted to studying the relationship that culture maintains with forces of technological, economic, political and institutional developments in a society. Largely, a product of the Euro-American social sciences, modernization paradigm of cultural studies was received in India with cautious criticism. Indian sociologists made their own conceptual and methodological innovations. A sharp distinction was drawn between westernization and modernization, locating this process in the cultural-historical individuality of each society and its initial historical conditions (Singh, 1973). The recognition of this factor was farsighted; the existence of plural traditions or patterns of modernization are today widely acknowledged even by its skeptics of the past (Eisenstadt, 1988). We encounter now several resurgent cultural responses to modernization, such as the Confucian, Islamic, Judaic and Hinduistic, in addition to the traditional Euro-Christian origin of this process in the past The caution of the Indian sociologists has been amply vindicated.

The system's boundary in the theory of cultural modernization was based upon the assumption of its inherent and universal rationality. Its edifice soon fell as the backwash effects of technological and industrial growth such as ecological decay, decline in family values, sharpening edges of the disguised exploitations, feelings of alienation among individuals and the disintegration in the structure and values of community life took alarming forms. This disenchantment from modernization probably added to the rise of the post-modernist debate, and its paradigms for the study of culture. Its precursor, the cultural analysis paradigm made innovations by studying culture in its symbolic depth; it focussed upon exploration of its latent codes, structures of meanings and semiotic forms. It does not reject totally the notions of structure or system. It, however, recognizes the variations and multiplicity of themes in the cultural space within a single community or a regional group (Singh, 1986). Post-modernism, on the other hand, rejects such assumptions in totality and seeks to explore culture by breaking the idea of system inside-out, and by the process of deconstruction of a culture's linguistic, spoken or written text. The post-modernist response to the study of culture rests in its method as well as in its critique of the aberrations of the contemporary post-industrial civilization. Or, is it itself a symptom of this aberration? However, the Indian sociologists are just beginning to evaluate it significance to the understanding of the cultural processes and it implications to social change.

It is a measure of the resilience of the Indian scholars that they have maintained an acute critical consciousness in respect of the new emerging paradigms of cultural studies originating in the West. Their focus has been on historicity of the Indian culture and civilization, towards indigenization of methods and theories and upon constructive criticism of paradigms of the western origin. This approach is intrinsic to the evolution of methods and theories for culture studies, and it has proved viable as now the uses of singular paradigm are being increasingly replaced by 'paradigm mixes' both in sociology and culturology (Erasov and Singh, 1991.)

CONTEMPORARY CULTURAL CHANGES

Many visible and significant cultural changes have taken place in India since independence. Across the nation, the lifestyle and leisure time activities of the people have changed. These include modes of consumption, styles of dress, uses of synthetic material or artefacts, modes of transport, and weakening of the traditional interdictions about the consumption of meat, poultry, etc. The consumption of fruits, vegetables and milk products now has a much wider base. The Green Revolution that took place in the 1970s is now supplemented by a White Revolution. The evidences provided by the Peoples of India (PoI) survey and the National Sample Surveys support the large extent of these changes. Where, on the one hand, ethnic and regional self-consciousness or identity of castes, tribes and minorities or other regional groups is increasing, there is evidence also to support the prevalence of many integrative cultural processes within our society which contribute to the growth of a holistic consciousness. There is increased inter-regional migration which makes it possible for regional cultural traits, culinary products, cultural performances, ritual forms, styles of dress and ornamentation to flow to other parts and mix together. The PoI has identified 91 cultural regions within India, almost each state having plural cultural regions with the possible exception of Goa "which forms a cultural zone" (Singh, 1992:53). The consumption profile of India which emerges from this survey, that of a total of 4,635 communities, belies the stereotyped image of India as being engrossed in "other-worldly asceticism" (Singh, 1992). In matters of consumption, the practice of non-vegetarianism is on the increase. Among some communities there is a parallel movement also towards vegetarianism. The use of alcohol is in vogue in some form or the other among about 50 per cent of the total communities in India. Of late, a rise in its consumption has become a matter of worry in several states and regions.

The emerging consumption profile of our people indicates, on the one hand, the cultural resilience of the past and the present aspects of our tradition, on the other hand, it also suggests as to how susceptible is our consumption behaviour to temptations of gross and unmindful consumerism. Even though relatively small, a substantial section of the upward mobile population in our society may be a victim of the consumerist temptations. A movement for balance and temperance is necessary. Notwithstanding this fact, the continuity of a high level of cultural resilience represented by a rising middle class, now more than 200 million in number, ensures product and market diversification so necessary for rapid economic growth. Considering its sociological features in our agrarian, industrial and service sectors of economy, this class may also discourage mindless consumerism having more proclivity towards savings and investments. The fragile balance between values and disvalues in lifestyle forms an area of continued education, and cautious vigilance in the society.

Integrative changes in our culture are also taking place in several other directions. Analysis of cultural values and practices of Indian communities in terms of culture traits indicates significant commonalities particularly within 'macro-regions'. Interestingly, these culture tracts are shared irrespective of differences in religion, caste and tribe. "There is very high correlation of traits between SCs and STs, between STs and Hindus, between Hindus and Sikhs and between Hindus and Muslims (which is very high indeed)", reports PoI survey. Many traits are shared by a large number of communities in India. In terms of language behaviour, there is phenomenal growth in bilingualism in India during the past two decades. The 1961 census estimated bilingualism to be 9.7 per cent, which grew to 13.4 per cent in 1971. The PoI survey estimates the extent of bilingualism at about 64.2 per cent. It signifies expansive growth in cultural interactions among people of different linguistic regions through migration, trade, communication exposures and cultural and social mobility of people.

ETHNICITY, CULTURAL IDENTITY AND CHANGE

Major occupational and techno-cultural changes have taken place in our society due to political, social and economic developments. These changes have promoted linkages and interactions among castes, tribes, religious groups and cultural regions. We notice significant magnitude of the spread effect of these cultural changes across regions and ethnic boundaries. These developments have, however, also reinforced people's self-consciousness and narrow cultural identities organized on principles of ethnicity, religion, caste, language and region. The process of cultural integration on national scale has grown but with simultaneous increase in search for cultural autonomy. We notice it among the tribes, not only as manifested in their political demands, but also in their movements, such as "return to tribal religion" despite their religion of conversion. Among the Dalits, there is a powerful movement for cultural autonomy. It reflects their long-standing disenchantment from Brahamanical caste-Hinduism (Singh, 1994: 71; Omvedt, 1993; Gore, 1993; Singh, 1973). The intensity of media exposure, political participation and competitive outlook towards social mobility have added strength to these processes. Politicization of religion is reflected in conscious distortions of meaning and uses of religious symbols, artefacts and rituals. The traits common among various religions of India are suppressed and those articulating distinction and separation are highlighted. There is increased tendency towards parochialization of culture or its symbolic forms.

In the context of overall social change, it is essential to examine the nature of relationships that demands for cultural autonomy or ethnicity have upon the processes of cultural integration in the Indian society as a whole. Sociological studies suggest the existence of a viable linkage between these two otherwise contradictory processes. Cultural integration of diverse entities in the pan-Indian society has had a long history. Its matrix was that of a civilization. This civilization was not subsumed in, but out-crossed religious, ethnic, linguistic and regional boundaries. It subsisted upon interdependence among diverse plural social entities established through technology, production processes, trade, market and circulation of products and of personnel engaged in pursuits of crafts, art, aesthetics, knowledge and learning. It was coincidental that Hinduism—the mainstream religion—contributed to the reinforcement of this civilization.

As Louis Renou (1953: 56) says: "Hinduism is a way of life, a mode of thought, that becomes second nature. It is not so much its practices that are important, for they can be dispensed with; nor is it the Church, since it has no priesthood, or at least no sacredotal hierarchy. The important thing is to accept certain fundamental conceptions, to acknowledge a certain 'spirituality', a term much abused in current parlance." It was possible for this religio-cultural mainstream to sustain or even thrive upon pluralities of religious faiths, practices and social groupings such as tribe, caste or minority faiths. Thus, diverse forms of cultural and social identities flourished under the diffuse umbrella of the Indian civilization. One identity or faith did not threaten the existence of the other.

The dispensation of cultural co-existence was founded upon a typical equilibrium established by a pre-industrial technology, mode of production and its social and political institutions. The two revolutions---one industrial and the other republican---have totally altered this traditional equilibrium. Industrial revolution generates demand for nation-building; it is followed by a search for a world community or global civilization. In the process of evolution through these two phases, the local and regional cultural identities feel threatened. The political process of nation-building and its economic-industrial correlates sharpen inequalities, at least in the initial phases; there is pressure for conformity and standardization in institutional relationships, such as economy, power structure, education, recreation, information and a whole range of the services. The more there is pressure for giving legitimacy to these macro-institutions, the more there is a sense of unease, often resentment, among localized cultural identities based on tribal, caste or religious groupings. Ironically, the fear of overarching national or global institutions has not subsided despite growth in economy and polity. The passage from industrial to post-industrial phase of social, economic and cultural development is not reassuring in several vital areas of human concerns, such as, the well-being of the basic institutions like family and community, the protection of the identity of cultural minorities, the practice of voluntaristic consensus methods in place of the uses of power or domination in cultural negotiations or decision-making and preservation of natural habitat of humankind and its quality.

India holds a unique position in the process of this transition. Here, we witness a conjuncture of cultural institutions and values belonging to the pre-industrial agrarian society with those which coincide with the cultural values of industrial capitalism. In a narrow, as yet a nascent form, we may also witness presence of symptoms of a post-industrial phase of cultural development in India. This makes the task of sociologists studying culture most exciting as well as most challenging. Happily, the social structure and institutions in our country have traditionally favoured preservation of cultural identities of the minority groups; the rich interaction between the folk and elite cultures ensured its success, and preserved cultural autonomy of plural identities in a loosely structured notion of a civilization. The cultural policies, implemented after independence, have in large measure been sensitive to the need for preservation of such identities. But, as we try to establish the national framework of an industrial society with potential to achieve the post-industrial phase of development, many pressures are generated, which may come to clash with the local cultural identities. It may generate anxiety or a threat perception at various levels of cultural organizations in our society.

COMMUNICATION, CULTURE AND ECONOMIC CHANGE

An important dimension of such perceptions is located in the contemporary processes of culture change in relation to the national paradigm of social and economic development. The past orientalist pronouncement, that Indian culture being otherworldly and fractured by segmentary divisions into caste, tribe, etc., would not help or rather hinder the growth of a modern economy and a democratic polity, has been proved erroneous. Castes, tribes, family institutions and religions, as illustrated by sociological studies, have richly contributed to the growth in agricultural and industrial entrepreneurship, and modern systems of profession, education, technology and science. The core values of the oral cultural tradition, which encouraged a culture of debates and articulation, and encouraged creative interaction with the written culture, proved helpful in indigenization of democratic values and integration of diversities. The absence of such cultural processes in the core values of a society may render the passage to democracy rather difficult to achieve (Chu, 1988:2-13). The oral tradition of the folk culture also reinforces the roots of cultural pluralism and preservation of local cultural identities. The core cultural values and institutions in India enshrined in the folk culture have served to strengthen the foundations of the Indian society, as they have interacted deeply with its literary or textual cultural traditions. This process integrates the micro-level of cultural institutions with those at the macro-level of institutionalization. There also exists a dialectical relationship between the literary tradition of the folk, Dalits and insurgents and the mainstream literary tradition (Singh, 1986:45) in contemporary India.

As we slowly enter into the industrial phase of capitalist development, several new cultural challenges are bound to be encountered, and most of these merit formulation of far-sighted policies. The massive entry of the mass media, the universalization of communication through radio and television, the proliferation in the number of English and vernacular language newspapers, journals, magazines, the technological availability of global information system through satellites, etc., are bringing about hitherto unknown degree of information-entertainment revolution. Mounted as this 'revolution' is on the chariot of market capitalism with propensity for endless profit-making, it may tend increasingly to convert culture into commodity. The emphasis may shift from content to packaging of culture. Not assimilation or integration of culture, but its marketing is an orientation which may usher culture into an unfamiliar domain, that of cut-throat competition with a market ethos. The revolution in information and communication technology, together with increase in the rapid means of transport, extended networking of markets of culture industries, such as tourism, inter-cultural meets and exchanges, institutionalized exchange of cultural objects, etc., contribute to globalization of culture. The process is bound to increase and exert ever new pressures as we march from industrial to post-industrial phase of development.

The new cultural challenges that these phenomena give rise to are many. It may augment the real as well as perceived threats to local and smaller cultural identities due to massification and marketization of culture. It may lead to non-institutionalized modes of inter-cultural contacts, such as through tourism, marketing of cultural objects, leisure enterprises such as hotels, tourist resorts, etc., that may be an imposition upon local or regional communities. In this process, the decontextualization and displacement of meanings and values of cultural objects may increase. Its impact upon values, cultural practices, ecology and mental and physical health and quality of life of the people may be disastrous. The consequent erosion of values and structures of folk culture, and decay in its creative relationship with the mainstream cultural tradition may be directly related to the growth in new leisure and culture markets. If, in the meantime, the traditional family system and the community or neighbourhood bonds weaken as it has happened in many developed societies, the new cultural changes portend major crisis in the social and cultural system of our society.

As of now our traditional social institutions such as family, caste, tribe, community and neighbourhood, etc., are able to throw up resilience. The Indian people have also shown cultural resilience in decodification of cultural meaning of symbols projected by mass media of communication They have largely behaved like, what is called an "active audience" or as "producers of meanings" (Schiller, 1988) from the messages in communication. The long exposure of the Indian middle classes to Euro-American culture through the uses of the English language, adds additional resilience to our exposure to the western cultural institutions. In the words of the Japanese social anthropologist Chie Nakane (1988:62), "if there is a meeting place of East and West, it is in India, not Japan". It may be a generous remark, but it has a basis in our history. However, despite our cultural resilience, the quality and institutional organization of the mass-based, market and commodity-oriented new cultural forces are most likely to cause dislocations. They may give rise to sub-cultures directly in conflict with the general cultural values or practices. Moreover, mass culture is backed by a faceless, striking power of technology and the massive organization of market capitalism (Dissanayake, 1988: 26-40).

The relevance of a cultural policy assumes significance in this context. Indeed, it is valid that the core and the creative domains of the culture of a people is the product of the spontaneous and innovative responses, both individual and collective, and it cannot be planned or orchestrated by a cultural policy. Nevertheless, in the context of cultural challenges that are most likely to be generated by the market capitalism, information technology and pressures of globalization of culture, a policy framework to meet the challenges becomes inevitable. In our country, such a cultural policy will have to be organically linked with the policies of our social and economic development. Probably, the urgent needs at one level, say cultural would have to be reflected at the other; for example, in the policy of economic globalization or liberalization. Broadly, such a policy framework must take into account the need to enrich and protect local and regional cultural values, practices and identities in the process of the cultural exposure to mega-institutions of mass communication and marketization.

No doubt, there is evidence to suggest that the expansion of electronic technologies such as computers and telecommunication, cultural systems with right level of economic growth and emphasis upon distributive processes for social mobility, resolves the problems of cultural identity, creates a sense of confidence or pride in people's heart in respect of their situation and, correspondingly, the fear of cultural dependency comes down or withers away. "Japanese experience indicates that a strong economy and superior technology tend to resolve rather than cause cultural identity problem." Moreover, "the cultural identity problem is considered to occur when cultural change is so drastic as to destroy the sense of continuity". Again, the "lesson drawn from Japanese experience is that the cultural identity problem is more strongly influenced by the present than the past, its origin or its history" (Youchi, 1988:196-201). The temporariness of creating new cultural identities by myth-making is also self-evident in India, but the Japanese experience suggests the need for a strong link among cultural policy, economic policy and technology policy.

In the process of creating this linkage, involvement of people, decentralization of decision-making process, uses of multimedia approach to communication of culture and value-sensitization of the market-oriented mega-cultural institutions and organizations would be necessary. Emphasis on plurality, identity and continuity is essential not only for a healthy direction and quality of cultural development in India, but also for its most effective role in bringing about social change in our society. A sudden discontinuity in culture can be politically destabilizing just as the lack of creative response to adapt and change can be stultifying and socially degenerative. A creative balance between continuity and change in cultural policy is, therefore, essential for us to achieve our future goal.

References

Chu, Leonard L. "In Search of an Oriental Communication Perspective" in *The World Community in Post-Industrial Society,* Volume 2 (ed.) Christian Academy, Seoul: Wooseok Publishing Co., 1988.

Disanayake, Wimal, "Communication, Knowledge and a Post-Industrial Society: The Need for a Value-Centred Approach", in Christian Academy (ed.), *The World Community in Post-Industrial Society,* Seoul: Wooseok Publishing Co., 1988.

Erasov, B. and Singh, Y., *The Sociology of Culture,* Moscow: Progress Publishers, 1991.

Eisenstadt, S.N., "How do Cultures of the East and the West Meet the Challenges of Acculturation in Global Industrialization? One or Several Modern Civilization?" in Christian Academy (ed.), *Encounter Between the East and the West and the Creation of a Global Culture,* Seoul: Wooseok Publishing Co., 1988.

Gore, M.S., *The Social Context of an Ideology,* New Delhi: Sage Publication, 1993.

Nakane, Chie, "Distance Between Cultures", in Christian Academy (ed.), *Encounter Between the East and the West and the Creation of a Global Culture,* Seoul: Wooseok Publishing Co., 1988.

Omvedt, Gail, *Dalits and the Democratic Revolution: Dr. Ambedkar and the Dalit Movement in Colonial India,* New Delhi: Sage Publication, 1994.

Renou, Louis, *Religion of Ancient India,* New Delhi: Munshiram Manoharlal, 1953.

Schiller, H., "Current Views of Information and Media Power", in Christian Academy (ed.), *Encounter Between the East and the West and the Creation of Global Culture,* Seoul: Wooseok Publishing Co., 1988.

Singh, K.S., *People of India: An Introduction,* Calcutta: Anthropological Survey of India, 1992.

—, *The Scheduled Tribes,* New Delhi: Oxford University Press, 1994.

Singh, Y., *Modernization of Indian Tradition,* Jaipur: Rawat Publications, 1973.

—, *Indian Sociology: Social Conditioning and Emerging Concerns,* New Delhi: Vistar Publishers, 1986.

—, *Social Change in India: Crisis and Resilience,* New Delhi: Har-

Anand Publications, 1993.

----, "Literature and Social Change: A Sociological Perspective", *Indian Horizons*, Volume XXVII, Number 3-4, 1988.

Unnithan, T. K.N., Indra Deva and Yogendra Singh, *Towards a Sociology of Culture in India*, New Delhi: Prentice Hall of India, 1965.

Youchi, Ito, "Beyond Cultural Dependency: A Japanese Case", in Christian Academy (ed.), *Continuity and Change in Communications in Post-Industrial Society*, Seoul: Wooseok Publishing Co., 1988.

2

Globalization and Local Cultures

Issues and Perspectives in India

There are two levels, theoretically, at which the relationship between the processes of globalization and the responses of the local cultures can be analyzed. Firstly, one has to recognize the near universal feeling of disenchantment in the social sciences from the totalizing and generalizing paradigms of positivism—a product of the European renaissance ideology. Positivism proposed abstract systems and categories of culture and society, which often proved inadequate in respect of fuller comprehension of reality. A more meaningful understanding of culture called for reflexive or empathic sensitivity in the concepts and methods of social science. Analytically, it has contributed to the growth in the phenomenological methods to study local cultures, and the use of ethno-methodological categories. A radical expression of the revolt against positivism is found in the post-modern rejection of the totalizing concepts of culture and social system. In the new approach, focus is upon the local, the particularistic and reflexive (Loyotard, 1987; Dilthey, 1988; also Earnst, G. 1992) dimensions of culture.

The significance of the 'local' in the interpretation of culture has also been theoretically recognized in social anthropology. It makes a departure from the 'etic' mode of the understanding of the 'other culture' to an 'emic' approach or a creative balance between the two perspectives (Geertz, 1975; Cohn, 1977). This approach in social anthropology offers the possibility in its paradigm to resolve the conceptual dichotomies of global versus local or historical versus nomological. It helps analytically to transcend the duality of the 'subject-object' in the study of culture. This orientation, which is not confined now to only social anthropology, has emerged from empirical-historical studies in history, sociology and other social sciences (Fox, 1971; Stokes, 1978; Stein, 1980). In India, the affirmation of this integrative paradigm in the studies of culture has come from the observational studies of the communities, the exploration of their 'oral' and the textual traditions and the studies of the local dynamics of culture and society.

Secondly, the need in social sciences to reformulate categories and methods to study culture has been necessitated by the technological revolution in the systems of communication, such as the increased uses of computers, telephony, Internet, etc., which have impacted deeply upon social institutions and modes of interaction. These have also revolutionized the institutions of finance and banking, trade and fiscal relationships, style of life and leisure activities. These changes created social, cultural and institutional forces which surpass the boundaries of the nation-state (Appadurai, 1996; Pieterse, 1996; Disanayake, 1988). Paradoxically, however, these changes impact upon the institutions of local culture and social forms such as the family, neighborhood and the community in a destabilizing manner and generate many forms of social anomie. At the same time, the universal reach of the communication media, such as the Internet, telephony, etc., have made it possible to produce and augment 'virtual localities' and 'virtual neighbourhoods', etc. Thus, the production of locality, as Arjun Appadurai terms it, goes hand in hand with the erosion of real-time and real-space bonds of communitarianism and local cultures. The disintegration of the folk culture and the folk societies due to marketization of economy and commoditification of production processes, through entrenchment of the capitalist mode of production in agriculture converts 'peasants' into 'farmers', eroding the traditional cultural patterns. It is evident, therefore, that in conceptual and theoretical terms, the relationship between the local culture and the processes of globalization should take into account both the analytical and substantive perspectives of the changing cultural realities.

THE INDIAN PERSPECTIVES

There exists a long tradition of research and analysis in India on the conceptual and substantive dimensions of culture at various levels of its existence: the local, the regional and the national. The national movement and the exposure to the western culture mediated by the colonial rule made Indians very self-conscious of their cultural identity. The anxieties about the impact of globalization and marketization of economy, media and information systems, the leisure and style of life etc., which have direct impact upon the symbolic contents and the foundations of the tradition, have today generated anxious debate among the scholars, the people and the political parties on the policy responses of the state. Such policy has long been in the making, but today the process of globalization and its impact on culture, both local and national, give it a new urgency (Singh, 1994). In most studies of cultural change in India the significance of locality and local culture and its relationship with the nation-state and the national culture has been widely recognized.

This is manifested from the sociology and social history of communities and cultures in India and the trends in the methods of their study. Significance of 'locality' and its role as the building-block of Indian culture and civilization has been increasingly accepted. And, as the processes of economic and social development have expanded, the importance of local cultures and the particularistic expressions of ideology and sentiments have been taken note of in formulation of the public policies as well as in the analysis of 'nation-state'. For instance, many studies of the communities and their social structure have consciously used people's perspective on social and cultural issues both for analysis of structures and policy formulations to induce change. Increasingly, emic method of analysis has been preferred to the etic mode which was dominating earlier (Mencher, 1978). Social historians have been making use of the emic paradigm as it was found to be particularly sensitive to locality-specific categories in the analysis of cultural reality. The contributions of Burton Stein (1980) and D. Ludden (1985) on the economic and social history of south India fall in this category. Stein brought out the significance of *nadu* (locality or region) in the governance of polity during the time of the Cholas (900-1000 A.D.). Ludden affirms the role of local communities and their autonomy in the operation of agrarian economy. This development in methodology marks also an integrative convergence of different paradigms of analysis of social reality. One could witness emerging convergence between the Marxist and the functionalist perspectives in many recent studies (Sivakumar and Sivakumar, 1977). The cultural and social boundedness of Indian culture by locality and region has long been recognized in the studies of caste, family and rural communities----the three basic social institutions of India. Caste and kinship ties even today have a marked regional and local cultural character (Singh, 1973; Oommen, 1997). These developments amply illustrate the recognition of plurality and locality in the analysis of Indian reality and in the social and economic policies for the transformation of society.

GLOBALIZATION, PLURALISM AND LOCAL CULTURE

The impact of globalization on local culture and the changing role of the nation-state can be examined by observing the particularities of the social and cultural patterns and their local, national and transnational manifestations in India. These social and cultural realities have a plural character in terms of language, geography, ethnicity, religion and culture. With partial exception of the tribal population, the caste system and its related kinship structures have shaped the profile of the culture, economy and power-structures within the local communities and regions. A recent all-India survey (PoI) of the communities, conducted by the Anthropological Survey of India, gives us an insight into the plurality of the caste-community structures and their cultural and socio-economic diversities. The basic category in this survey is 'community' which is conceptually used as "in ethnography, which is marked by endogamy, occupation and perception" (Singh, 1992:23). The term 'community' as used in the survey resembles the concept of caste-tribe, though it is not exhaustive of all their features. It's findings illustrate how the local cultures and their particularities do not infringe upon establishing linkages between the local culture and the national culture and consciousness in India.

Communities have been identified at various levels: firstly, there are very large categories of communities including castes and the minorities; secondly, those that identify themselves through linguistic and cultural categories (e.g., Assamese, Bengali, Gujarati, Rajasthani, Tamil, etc); and thirdly, while the communities have been identified in terms of endogamy, occupation and social perceptions, there are about half a dozen communities which do not conform to the three-fold criteria (Singh, 1992:51). The fourth type of communities are those identified as Adi Dharma, Adi Andhra, Adi Karnataka, etc., falling under the constitutional list of the scheduled castes. In all, there are 4,635 communities in India. These are spread into 2,209 main communities and 586 segments of these communities are estimated through other sources. Added to these main communities and their main segments, the other communities and their segments spread all over the states and union territories give a total of 4,635 communities.

The state-wise distribution of communities gives us an indication of the density of local culture as measured by the diversity in the number of communities. In this context, the survey states:

> "The communities are unevenly distributed in all states and union territories including Bay Islands. By far the largest number of communities (above 350) are found in Andhra Pradesh and Tamil Nadu. They vary from 250-350 in Uttar Pradesh, Bihar, Madhya Pradesh, Maharashtra, Orissa, Karnataka and Gujarat. The range varies from 150-250 in West Bengal, Rajasthan and Kerala. Arunachal Pradesh, Assam, Tripura, Jammu & Kashmir, Himachal Pradesh, Haryana and Punjab have communities ranging from 50-150. The number of communities drops to below 50 in Nagaland, Manipur, Mizoram, Meghalaya, Sikkim, Goa, Chandigarh and Bay Islands' (Singh, 1992).

The range of distribution of communities in the states/union territories as portrayed by the PoI survey affirms the findings of anthropologists who studied the 'caste elaboration' in India as measured by a number of castes in rank order spread over a region. Their findings indicated that the elaboration of caste was very high in the states of southern peninsula of India; it was weaker in the periphery of the eastern (West Bengal) and the western (Punjab, Haryana) states in India; and of course, it did not find to any significant extent the presence of caste in the tribal states of India, such as Mizoram, Meghalaya, Manipur, Nagaland, etc. (Marriott, 1965; Singh, 1973) Sociologically, therefore, a close structural and cultural relationship between caste and community is established. It largely avers the proposition that the diversity of local cultures and their social context is located in the pluralism of castes, tribes and linguistic-religious and regional communities.

An important question that arises from this profile of cultural pluralism pertains to the extent of its relationship or linkages with the macro-structure of the nation-state. In other words, to what extent are the cultural and social forces generated within the communities, tribes and castes divisive or integrative for the structural identity and consciousness of the nation-state. The findings of the PoI survey affirm that the diversity of communities does not reduce the nature of sociological reality of states/union territories. More than 71 per cent of the communities are located within the boundaries of states/union territories. This shows that our states/union territories are not only linguistic and cultural but also 'sociological categories'. There are only 111 (3.97 per cent) communities that are spread all over India. Interestingly, diversity of communities exists not only among the Hindus but among the minority religions too. The communities found within minority religions are: Muslims-584, Sikhs-130, Jains-100, Buddhists-93, Christians-339, Jews-7, Parsis-3 and Animism-411. This explains the diversity and complexity of social structures and cultural practices among various religious groups, as it also affirms the essential plurality of cultures and cultural practices in India.

This diversity of local cultures is, however, also characterized by linkages and shared commonalities of culture traits, rituals, beliefs and customs. Studies of folk culture across regions, as distant as Uttar Pradesh from Rajasthan, have shown remarkable similarity in the ritual styles, songs and their central themes and symbols. The processes, both of universalization (integration) and parochialization, have been simultaneously going on in India in respect of sacred rituals, myths, legends and their symbolic representations (Singh, 1973; Unnithan et al., 1965; Erosov and Singh, 1991) over the millennia. The PoI survey maintains this reality by identifying 91 cultural regions on the basis of the distribution of culture traits among the communities. It concludes: "Within the majority of states there are a number of cultural regions marked by a distinct language/dialect, territorial identity, cultural variations and varying levels of economic growth. There are also small states like Goa which form a cultural zone. There are 91 such cultural regions where we have studied the communities" (Singh, 1991:53). The fact that the local cultures of castes, ethnicity and communities dispersed into over four thousand entities lend itself to regionalization of culture zones into 91 configurations affirms the presence of linkage and interaction between the local and trans-local cultural manifestations.

The local and regional cultures are also manifested through linguistic diversity of India. Language which intimately symbolizes the basis of culture has been an important issue in defining the territorial boundaries of the Indian states soon after independence. It was assumed that a linguistic region implied greater cultural homogeneity in respect of most other culture traits, practices and values. A State Reorganization Commission was set up with the objective of suggesting new boundaries of the states in India based on the principles of linguistic cultural affinity keeping in view the broad objective of unity and security of India and also factors related to the economic and administrative viabilities. The states were reorganized following the recommendations of the Commission as far as possible.

This has, however, not fully resolved the demands of regional and sub-regional aspirations. The linguistic-cultural affinity does not seem to contain the totality of the shared culture traits in a region. Several minority linguistic groups or those speaking through dialects seek more established status and demand separate states for themselves. Several such linguistic cultural movements are going on in India. Among the major movements are the Jharkhand movement in Bihar, the Gorkhaland movement in West Bengal and the Uttarakhand movement in Uttar Pradesh. There are many other movements in the making based on similar ideology. These are either an off-shoot of the past bases of the state reorganization or a result of new aspirations growing due to awareness of a sense of deprivation arising out of the uneven levels of economic, political and social growth in various states (Oommen, 1997; 1986).

The PoI survey lists 325 languages spoken by communities in India. About 33 languages are spoken by about 3,263 communities belonging to all the three social categories, viz., the scheduled castes, the scheduled tribes and the other communities. It illustrates how linguistic cultural sharing among tribes and castes and other communities is quite strong within the strands of pluralism. There is another set of 31 languages which are shared only by the scheduled castes and other communities, but not by the scheduled tribes. These languages are spoken in about 705 communities. The other sets of languages which are spoken singly either by the scheduled tribes or the scheduled castes or other communities are quite large and the number of communities speaking these languages is about 1,371, dispersed all over the country. It can be presumed that the deprivations on account of linguistic-cultural minority status, such as with regard to development of script, recognition for radio broadcast, television broadcast and other privileges, these communities may reflect higher degree of sensitivity. Correspondingly, the linguistic groups belonging to the first category (33 languages spoken by 3,263 communities) should be prone more to play dominant role in political and cultural mobilization. The same could be said for the second group of 31 languages spoken by 705 communities belonging to the scheduled castes and other communities. Indeed, political movements for the formation of separate state or for constitutional recognition of the language, etc., are going on within the communities belonging to this linguistic category.

It is evident how the linguistic diversity does not necessarily imply cultural particularism for most communities in India. The increasing incidence of bilingualism in India reinforces this evidence. Bilingualism was estimated rather conservatively at 13.4 per cent in 1971 census', while it was recorded to be at the level of 64.2 per cent by PoI survey in 1991. Increased linguistic interaction among tribes and non-tribes is leading to 'creolization of linguistic usages, and 58.91 per cent communities listed in the Constitution of India are now bilingual. Obviously, even the linguistic particularism has evolved a mode of operation in

India which extends linkages in the domain of culture to a wider set of communities at the regional and national levels.

Cultural particularism manifests itself integratively at many other levels. The distribution and sharing of culture traits among communities in India shows a "high correlation of traits among states within macro-regions such as those in the south, north-western India, central and western India and so on". Among social and religious groups, "there is very high correlation of traits between the SCs (scheduled castes) and the STs (scheduled tribes), between STs and Hindus, between Hindus and Sikhs, between Hindus and Muslims (which is very high indeed), and between Hindus and Jains. The high correlation between Hindus and Buddhists may also be explained in the same way. The fact that these communities interact across space or states is important" (Singh, 1992: 99). Despite these linkages, however, occasional conflict among the communities cannot be ruled out since all culture traits (about 776 of them) do not carry equal value.

The traits related to religion, power and dominance, for instance, carry more weightage and maladjustment in these domains may lead to conflict or even violence. It is, however, revealed that over a period of time interaction and interrelationship among the social and religious groups has increased in the fields of occupation, connubialities, services and professions etc. The traditional linkages persist and many modern linkages have emerged. There exists a high degree of perception of mobility both in terms of space and consciousness among Indians. The PoI survey concludes: "The picture of India that emerges, in spite of conflicts and contradictions, is also one of sharing of environment and ethos by communities and of their vibrant participation in political and economic processes and ritual roles. These facts explain why there has generally been a continuity and why a sense of harmony prevails over a large part of the countryside in spite of conflicts that some time threaten to tear our social fabric apart and why return to normalcy is often quicker after every searing experience. India is also a land of the migrants. There are very few communities which do not consider themselves to be migrants. Every community recalls its migration to the native habitat in its folklore and history. The whole of India is a *kshetra* (field) and an Indian is a migrant par excellence" (Singh, 1992: 100-103).

Globalization, as a process, has far-reaching cultural potential. India, which still remains largely a nation of peasants and working classes totalling about 70 per cent of population, renders the influence of the institutional structures of globalization to some extent self limiting. The process is further constrained due to illiteracy of about 40 per cent of population. Nevertheless, a very high rate of growth of the middle classes now ranging between 150 and 200 million has taken place. It offers vitality and opportunity to the forces of globalization. It also exposes the new social cultural and economic forces of globalization to contradictory impulses of acceptance and rejection. Today, this dualism acutely defines the limits of globalization in Indian society. There are strong social, political and cultural movements that are extremely suspicious of new institutions and linkages which globalization brings into wake in society. Yet, there is substantial population which does not shy away from the cultural, social, technological and economic linkages and institutions which follow globalization. A large majority of the middle classes are supportive of this process.

The global culture and its impact on Indian society has been widely discussed (Kothari, 1995, 1995b; Singh, 1994; Krishna Kumar, 1996; Peggy Mohan, 1995) in the recent social science publications. The new institutional innovations that globalization may bring about in society are: market, trade and finance, communication and media, technology and science, migration and inter-cultural transactions. There are related issues of tourism, mobility of professionals and the emergence of diasporic sub-cultures. In social structural terms, globalization is a historical process of transition from the agrarian-industrial, post-industrial and finally the stage of the information society (Dissanayake, 1988). To evaluate the implications of globalization on the local cultures and social and political institutions, it will be necessary to examine the implications that the major institutional organs of globalization have upon some of these institutions in India.

CULTURAL IMPACT OF GLOBAL TRADE AND MARKET

The scope of trade and market which are accelerated by the processes of globalization poses formidable cultural problems in both the developed and the developing societies. In India, which traditionally had quite a developed pre-industrial base of trade and market, the impact of the changing role of these institutions has been gradual. The market and trade relations continue to be located in local cultures even today (Ostor, 1980). Also, the economic policy of India upto the 1980s has been that of import-substitution and protectionism in trade and market. The full momentum of the globalization of economy started from 1990s onwards, but many checks and balances continue to persist. Nevertheless, this historical change in policy has impacts upon local cultures deeply in addition to having an overall cultural impact on the society. The new changes have been noticed in the lifestyle, consumption pattern, production of cultural objects and their circulation (marketing) and usages, in the cultural ecology and habitat and the religious practices etc. These changes have altered the traditional modes of cultural expressions, usages of language and communication media at the local, regional and national levels. These have also created many sub-cultures of an entirely new kind in the urban areas. The rise of popular culture is a new phenomenon with linkages both in the rural and urban centres.

Most of these changes have long been in the process of emergence and crystallization. The forces of industrialization and developments in agriculture had a major impact upon the consumption style of people. The Green Revolution in agriculture during the 1970s gave spurt to changes in the consumption style of villagers which till then was largely a preserve of the residents in cities and metropolises. Various rounds of the surveys conducted by the National Sample Survey (NSS) between 1972-73 and 1987-88, and the PoI survey of communities by the Anthropological Survey of India, amply testify to the changing patterns of consumption and lifestyle, both in the urban centres and the countryside. The NSS data show noticeable decline in the consumption of cereals both by the rich and the poor in India. The shift is towards consumption of milk, poultry and meat products. It is a phenomenon universal to the process of economic development. Indeed, between 1972-73 and 1987-88, the consumption of cereals in urban India averaged around 11.2 kilograms per capita per month and that in rural India it declined from 15.3 to 14.5 kilograms per capita per month. This decline is a part of a secular change in the composition of the Indian diet; consumers, both rich and poor, are spending relatively more on the non-cereal food such as milk and meat than on the cereals. Some authors have argued that such shifts in expenditure shares are not merely a reflection of increased prosperity; rather food preferences have been changing over time (Meenakshi, 1996; Radhakrishnan and Ravi, 1992). There is ample evidence about a change in the people's tastes in matters of consumption.

Rapid changes have also taken place at other levels of the consumption pattern and lifestyle. The electrification in villages has changed the energy-use pattern, particularly in the sub-urban villages; in remote villages, the use of firewood and cowdung is still common, although "the tribals are less dependent on cowdung than other communities. Sawdust is a new source of energy. The use of kerosene oil is widespread. Gobar gas plants have yet to make a major impact, and the use of solar energy has only made a beginning" (Singh, 1992:93). The expansion of road networks and means of communication has brought about some homogenization in tastes and consumption patterns, such as increased popularity of tea, coffee, egg, meat and fish. Following the Green Revolution, the country is now going through a White Revolution being the largest gross producer of milk in the world. The per capita consumption of milk, however, remains still inadequate. The use of synthetic materials for utensils, jars and cans is now common. Yet, most such artifacts still maintain ethnic tastes and designs and the traditional forms. A remarkable change in the style and pattern of women's wear has taken place. It is marked by a shift from *saris* to *salwar-kameez* (a traditional dress of Punjab now spread all over the country). The middle classes are increasingly taking to uses of designer dresses marketed by the multinationals. The uses of cosmetics, soaps and detergents have reached all sections of the people in India. The vocation of beauticians, and the number of beauty parlours and health clubs, etc., have grown very rapidly. These are no longer a preserve of the metropolises or the rich classes, they have moved even to relatively small towns in various parts of the country. The changes are more remarkable in the lifestyles of youth and the adolescents, but the elderly are not totally apathic or untouched by these changes.

Such changes are not entirely alien to the traditional Indian values. The PoI survey records high incidence of meat-eating, smoking and drinking in India and it is continuously growing. The culture of asceticism or self-denial was confined to a small section of the puritan upper castes and priests throughout the tradition. Culturally, therefore, the new changes may not have deeply subversive effect upon the core traditional values or the worldview of the people. Yet, one witnesses periodic incidence of consumer resistance against multinationals promoting new consumer goods or agro-products; e.g., sporadic movements against products like McDonald's hamburger and Kentucky fried chicken; farmers are resisting the penetration of agro-multinationals in the production of seeds, herbs, new cereals, etc. The cultural history of modern India reveals, however, that such movements are not entirely new. Their dimension and orientation is no doubt changing with globalization as these have an impact upon the cultural identity of the nation in an entirely new mode of historical experience.

The changes in consumption and lifestyle have been accelerated by the market forces and their changing structure. India has had a developed private market network since centuries in the past. Today, markets are not only extensive in their network, they also perform qualitatively new functions. The PoI survey notes: "Market forces have become all-pervasive with members of 94 per cent of communities reporting direct links with it." It also concludes that monetization of economy is now almost complete with only 2 per cent of communities, mostly tribal, reporting barter. With such an extensive network of markets and with changing style of living, the challenges of globalization to local culture in India assume deeper significance. A part of the change is related to the shift in occupation which has occurred in a very substantial measure. There no longer exists a link between caste or community and the hereditary occupation. The average number of occupations per community stands at 5.3, of which 1.8 is traditional and 3.5 is the newly acquired occupation (Singh, 1992: 89). Economists have also observed substantial rise in non-agricultural occupations in the countryside due mainly to the changes in the style of life consequent upon increased uses of consumer durables such as bicycles, motor-cycles, jeeps and electronic devices like radio, television and audio/video systems. Links with roads, railways and proliferation of developmental institutions have further augmented this process.

Markets are the vital mechanisms through which globalization extends its reach. Globalization is, however, just in a state of beginning in India. Some of its effects upon the regional and national cultures may be modernizing but there are significant areas where it has a disruptive influence upon the local cultures. For example, globalization of markets has led to conversion of traditional objects of art and aesthetics having mostly ritual uses in the local communities into marketable commodities. This has not only rapidly disrupted the autonomy of folk cultures, but also destablized the life of the artisans by creating new networks of competition and price war and a new class of exploitative middle men. In other areas, such as access of local communities to forest resources, land and rivers, hills and lakes, all of which were bounded together in a long enduring cultural ecology of rituals and customs, the penetration of market for profit has started a rapid subversion of ecology. It has disrupted the balance in the cultural, social and economic life of many communities including tribes, artisans, traditional cultural performers, etc. Being in minority and economically vulnerable, these communities suffer loss of their cultural identity the most in the process of globalization.

GLOBALIZATION OF COMMUNICATION, MEDIA AND LOCAL CULTURES

Most revolutionary aspect of cultural, social and economic globalization is reflected in the advances in technology of communication. The electronic media of communication such as radio, television, computer networks via satellites, paging services, telephony, electronic mail and Internet web, etc., are modes of communication which are revolutionizing the banking, trade and management practices, uses of culture and leisure, and most other modes of inter-cultural and inter-group communicative actions. It is possible to have individual to individual, group to individual and group to group communication contacts globally. Most of these media transcend the territorial national cultural boundaries. They may function beyond the sovereignty of the nation-state, and offer individuals enormous amount of choices and freedom in matters of cultural and ideological preferences. The notions of time, space and symbolism of culture undergo new transformation of meanings under the impact of these new telecommunication technologies. Its impact on cultures---local, regional and national---is multifaceted and can be integrative as well as disruptive. Moreover, these changes play a strategic role in the process of social, economic and technological development of society.

For centuries India remained largely an 'oral society'. The oral mode of communication played a major role in its freedom movement, the incidence of illiteracy being very high. This even today remains at the level of about 40 per cent . The print media soon added a new dimension to communication process. The first newspaper in English was published in 1780 from Calcutta. The colonial policies placed many restraints on publication of newspapers and their circulation. After independence, the Indian Constitution guaranteed its citizens "the right to freedom of speech and expression", and the new policies about the press were evolved by a series of Press Commissions. The Press Commission of 1980 was enjoined upon to suggest "the role of the press in the development of a democratic society; constitutional and legal safeguards to protect citizen's right to privacy; press as an industry, social institution, and forum for initiating discussion on public affair" (Das, 1997). The Press Commission recommended the establishment of a Newspaper Development Commission (NDC) to promote development of Indian languages news agencies, and to oversee their financial health; to provide development assistance to the press, especially to the small and medium newspapers; and to assist the emergence and growth of daily newspapers in remote and interior areas. Thus, the policy has been oriented to the protection and development of local and regional linguistic and cultural aspirations and interests.

India has now established a vigorous tradition of freedom of press through a vast number of newspapers and periodicals. In 1993, the total number of newspapers in circulation was 33,612; of them 3,740 were dailies, 275 tri/bi weeklies, 11,136 weeklies and 18,461 other periodicals (Das, 1997:19). There are various institutional agencies to support and monitor issues and needs related to the press. There also exists the Press Information Bureau which provides accreditation to the journalists numbering 1,322. News agencies like Press Trust of India (PTI) and United News of India (UNI) have global linkages and provide news to papers. The non-aligned news agencies pool (NAMEDIA) came into existence in 1976 for exchange of news among the non-aligned countries. In addition, there are several other agencies and services provided by the government to promote newspapers in India.

Besides the major telecommunication means, viz., radio, television and films, the role of telephones, mobilephones, e-mail, fax, Internet, etc., is also expanding. The radio, even today, continues to be the most accessible mass-based medium. In 1997, it had 187 stations, 297 transmitters and covered 94.5 per cent of population. It broadcasts educational, developmental, informative and entertainment oriented programmes in almost all regional languages of India. In addition, it also broadcasts programmes of national interest including regular news. There are local, regional and national channels, besides an external services division, which cater to various types of entertainment, information and developmental needs of expatriates. Specific programmes for children, women, farmers and on matters related to health, sports, etc., have a priority in radio broadcasts. There is emphasis on promotion of both classical cultural forms of music, dance and drama etc. as well as the folk, regional and local cultural formats. But, the popularity of film-based songs and dance sequences remains on the top. Such programmes are beamed by both radio and television.

Films have played a very important role in India, and even today remain the most popular form of entertainment and recreation. They have also played a crucial part from time to time in promoting educational and reformative values. They have proved to be a major source of linguistic and cultural integration. To regulate their content and form in tune with the normative standards of society the government has established a Central Board of Film Certification. In 1996 alone 683 films were produced in 23 languages including Spanish. The five major languages in which maximum number of films are produced include: Hindi (126), Tamil (138), Telugu (154), Kannada (86) and Malayalam (65). Films have also been produced in languages of the smaller communities reflecting local or regional cultures such as Manipuri, Konkani, Urdu, Garhwali, Rajasthani, etc. The Indian Television, also known as Doordarshan, draws heavily from film-based programmes. Doordarshan, which made a modest beginning in 1968 with the objective of showing educational programmes for social and economic development of society, has rapidly expanded during the last two decades of the present century. With the availability of satellite facilities it runs three types of transmitters: very high power (77), low power (534) and very low power (153).

Between 1982 and 1995, India launched eight INSAT-series satellites which have contributed to a massive expansion of the Doordarshan coverage to 846.5 million of the total population (Annual Report, I&B Ministry, 1996-97). Doordarshan now has eight channels: DD-1, which beams national, regional, local and educational programmes, DD-2, which is an entertainment channel, DD-3, which is the infotainment channel with programmes on culture and current affairs, Regional Languages Satellite Service (RLSS) which offers programmes to promote regional and local languages, the DD-India, which offers international services to 50 countries, the DD Movie Club and DD-CNNI offering 24 hours current affairs programmes. In addition, there is state network which beams Hindi programmes to concerned states. Now, about 60 million homes have TV sets with viewership of 415 million. Doordarshan has maintained more than 80 per cent viewership in urban areas and 95 per cent in rural areas despite opening of the foreign channels.

With new impetus towards globalization of telecommunication, the Videsh Sanchar Nigam Ltd. (VSNL) has been established which administers policies approved by the government in the domain of global communication. It is an autonomous corporation with government holding 82.02 per cent of the shares. It offers service of cellular telephone with roaming facilities---regionally, nationally and internationally. It had launched the Internet service in India in 1995 which at present has about 10,000 subscribers. It expects rapid growth in the coming years (one estimate is that it will go upto 50,000 by 2000 A.D.). There are only 5 million computers in the country as of now. The growth has been slow, but it is likely to pick up fast. The VSNL expects to meet the expanded telephony demands which was raised from 3,331 in 1992 to 12,873 in 1996 and further to 35,000 in 1997. It also expects the terrific growth in telecommunication at the rate of 21 per cent, much above the international rate in the coming years (Annual Report, VSNL, 1995-96). India, with its new policy of liberalization and privatization of telecommunication, is now moving fast towards global linkages---economic, cultural and social.

But, the question is: how does the globalization process in mass communication impact upon the local and national cultures? How do local cultures respond to the challenges and exposures to new cultural values, styles of life and institutional norms? The experience in this field so far does not suggest that the impact is entirely negative. There is clear evidence that electronic mass communication has revolutionized economic growth, trade and banking practices and exchange of information in health, management, profession, etc., leading to new growth possibilities. These are making growth-related outputs with global linkages. The new means of communication also augment and empower the local communities, local cultures and minority sects by extending the reach of their interactions. Their cultural and emotional bonds are strengthened due to their global reach through new telecommunication linkages, e.g., video-meetings, tele-discussions, etc. The new media also creates 'virtual' communities and cultural enclaves by offering the possibility of sustained communicative interaction among members scattered in far off places (Appadurai, 1996; Annual

Report, VSNL, 1995-96).

Apart from such empowering impact, the local communities and cultures are also inspired by the new telecommunication media to reassert their cultural identity and reinforce their resilience. It helps them maintain their identity by accessing themselves to cultural meanings and values rather selectively through an adaptive mechanism. No doubt, the mass media convert members of communities into audience; but often the audience reacts to messages not passively, it decodifies the cultural symbols and messages 'actively' as "producers of meanings" (Schiller, 1988). This is particularly true in India where in course of three decades of exposure to mass culture of films, radio, television, video, etc., the self-consciousness of the local cultures and communities has not diminished. It has become more articulate about its identity and interests. Globalization, therefore, not only makes people's sense of cultural identity and cultural values more caring of a shared existence within diversity, but it also makes them highly critical and conscious about the 'hidden packages' of self-serving ideologies in communication. We find it in the context of market values which draw enormous strength through globalization without commensurate moderation of its propensity to profit and exploitation.

OTHER PROCESSES OF GLOBALIZATION

Globalization, both of economy and information systems, accelerates the processes of migration, tourism and travel. Its cultural and social homogenizing effects proceed along with creation of pluralism and cultural diversity. Cultural diaspora is created by migrants settling down in countries which offer them better income and employment opportunities. The studies of the Indian outmigrants suggest that most of them continue to maintain their traditional ways of life and customs. More than this, their cultural self-awareness becomes more protective and strengthens their commitment to the traditional modes of culture even more than in the country of their origin. Cultural tourism, both as an organized industry and as a source of leisure or recreation, gains momentum as communication and travel facilities are modernized.

The diaspora communities have existed in India since a very long time. Many Indians settled down in Mauritius, Fiji, Surinam, etc., as indentured workers of the British planters. Indians also travelled to East Asian countries as cultural messengers, and to Africa and Central Asia for trade and commerce. They migrated later to USA, Britain and Canada for employment and education. Currently, we have an Indian diaspora spread almost all over the world, but it seems to be more concentrated in UK, USA, UAE, Saudi Arabia and Canada as indicated from the communicative interactions. In rank order, these five countries were on top in telephone calls, both incoming and outgoing, in India during 1995-96 (Annual Report, VSNL, 1995-96). Tourism is comparatively a less developed industry. In 1995, India received 17,49,397 foreign tourists; this figure did not exceed 2 million upto 1997. Yet, tourism does pose the problems of cultural intrusion on the local cultures in selected high-intensity tourist spots, e.g., in Rajasthan, Goa, Uttar Pradesh and Karnataka. In most of these, states the cultural impact of the foreign tourists is viewed with suspicion; there is need for an integrated planning. A more promising and larger area of tourism is domestic tourism which remains underdeved so far. Domestic tourism is estimated to grow upto 134 million in numbers in near future (Archana Singh, 1997). This tourism is oriented more to religious pilgrimages combined with sight-seeing and for leisure. It is, therefore, culturally reinforcing and integrative. There has been an immense proliferation of sacred places of all religious groups during the past four decades. This has strengthened the festive and celebrative activities of various religious groups and communities and its diffusion effect has been strong. Each religious group, including the minorities, now increasingly celebrates their cults and festivals on a much larger scale than ever before by taking the advantages of the new means of communication.

POLITY, INTEGRATION AND IDENTITY

The process of globalization has triggered off forces of change which have set people rethinking about the political institutions such as the state, the democracy and the civil society. In their functioning, the role of cultural pluralism and protection of the local cultures is now particularly recognized both in terms of institutional mechanism and as an element of political morality or value system. New thinking is taking place about the changing role of nation-state, its sovereignty and the role of political party, etc., under the growing forces of globalization (Kothari, 1995; Sartori, 1991; Apter, 1991; Keane, 1991). The changing relationship between the state and the civil society, following globalization of economy and pluralization of cultures, now poses a major problem in most societies, both developed and the developing (Hirst and Khilnani, 1996; Singh, 1997). New issues about the future policy for the democratic states have also emerged.

The Indian Constitution, adopted soon after independence, defines the rights and privileges of castes, minorities, tribal groups and the weaker sections of society. These are covered by the fundamental rights as well as the directive principles of the state policy. The policy of positive discrimination favouring the weakest communities amongst the caste groups, the tribes and the backward classes has been implemented covering about 50 per cent of the population. Reservations are provided for these communities in educational institutions, political offices and government services. The tribal policy of the government has consistently aimed at encouraging their autonomous growth with protection to their local culture. To protect their rights in land and forest resources, etc., the law prohibits outsiders from purchasing their property or to settle down on their land by purchasing estate which is their preserve. There is an innerline protection policy pursued by the government which protects tribals from intrusion by outsiders from other states or the foreigners. Cultural autonomy and rights of the minorities to pursue their religion and cultural practices are constitutionally guaranteed. The tribals and weaker sections are also protected by law. They enjoy privileges in running their own educational, cultural and social institutions.

These measures have, however, been less successful in maintaining the autonomy of the tribal local cultures. There is evidence that outside entrepreneurs, traders and influential people have succeeded in alienating the land and natural resources meant for the tribals by surreptitious means. The educational standard, economic status and political empowerment of the tribal communities has, therefore, remained low in most regions of the country. However, as the functioning of the democratic forces has become stronger, a resentful local leadership has emerged among these communities sponsoring movements either for a separate state, or political autonomy or even separation from the union (Oommen, 1997). Nevertheless, it is observed that the preservation of the identity of the local cultures, either from the market forces or predatory classes or an activist state, has so far been possible by the strength of the democratic forces. During the past few decades, these forces have progressively gained more and more strength giving impetus to movements towards strengthening the institutions of the civil society. The role of the non-governmental agencies has been pivotal in this process. Lately, a policy for decentralization of power to the village panchayats has been enacted by a constitutional amendment. It empowers the village communities and gives them autonomy in many areas of economic, social and cultural developmental administration. Women have been accorded 33 per cent reservation in the council of the village panchayats, thus for the first time empowering them to have a more decisive role in formulation and implementation of policies.

Globalization, market economy and powers of the media or information technologies are bound to put pressures on the local cultures. Some degree of acceleration towards homogenizing of cultural forms and activities can also be envisaged. Its consequences to the local communities may be progressive or developmental if the disintegrative tendencies which these forces generate are minimized. Though difficult, this task may not be impossible to accomplish. There are several reasons for this. First, the social structure and cultural system in India are intrinsically based on pluralism and diversity. The caste society and tribes are segmented into communities (about 4,635 according to PoI survey) which in the form of local groups or entities enjoy enormous cultural autonomy. M.N. Srinivas (1996) rightly concludes: "Indian culture is characterized by enormous diversity. It would not be an exaggeration to say the cultural situation in India varies every few miles. And even within a single village each caste has culture which is somewhat different from that of the other. In fact, it would not be an exaggeration to state that each kinship unit has its own distinctive cultural practices, representing a fusion of different incoming affinal strands modifying the culture of the main agnatic stem." This provides enormous cultural resilience to communities in India to filter the effects of globalization through refractory and prismatic adaptations. This also provides unique resilience to local cultures. However, the local cultures, either of castes or tribes, also have linkages with other castes and tribal communities at many levels of functioning. This is what defines the unity of India within diversities.

The second source of resilience to local cultures is the institution of democracy. Dispersed into half a million villages, Indians have by tradition enjoyed the power of cultural autonomy. A system of continual and effective dialogue and debate has been the most characteristic feature of an average Indian's conduct. This is probably one of the additional reasons why the roots of democracy are deeper in India. Its core values of debate and dissent evolving into consensus give it a native advantage in the acceptance of democratic values (Singh, 1994; Chu, 1988). Globalization, it is argued, erodes country's political sovereignty (Appadurai, 1996). Some scholars contest this proposition on the assumption that globalization without democratization may enhance inequalities and forces of neocolonialism with unpredictable consequences (Chatterjee, 1997). This view also assumes a disjunction between democracy and civil society. As we have explained, the intrinsic features of the social structure and patterns of culture in India do not favour a disjunction between the two---conclusion derived from the historicity of the western societies.

Finally, it has been experienced that every step of movement towards economic, political and cultural modernization, taken by the state in India, is responded to by the people with an enhanced sense of self-consciousness and awareness of identity. Cultural modernization, sponsored by the forces of globalization, is resented if it encroaches upon or does not promote the core cultural values of society, its language, social practices and styles of life. The vigour of the renewed sense of self-awareness generated among the members of the local cultures and communities is such as to succeed in making adaptive reconciliation with the forces of globalization. The linkages both visible and invisible, defining the cultural interdependence among communities and regions in India which have existed historically, reinforce instead of threatening the national identity. These bonds seem to become stronger as India encounters the forces of modernization and globalization.

References

Appadurai, Arjun, *Modernity at Large : Cultural Dimensions of Globalization*, Minneapolis: University of Minnesota Press, 1996.

Chatterjee, Partha, "Beyond the Nation? Or Within?", *Economic and Political Weekly*, January 4-11, 1977.

Chu, Leonard, L., "In Search of an Oriental Communication Perspective", in Christian Academy (ed.), *World Community in Post-Industrial Society : Continuity and Change in Communications in Post-Industrial Society*, Seoul: Wooseok Publishing Co., 1988.

Cohn, B.S., "African Models and Indian Histories", in R.G. Fox (ed.), *Realm and Region in Traditional India*, New Delhi: Vikas Publishers, 1977.

Das, Biswajit, "Mass Media", Report on Fifty Years of Communication Growth in India, Mimeographed, 1997.

Dilthey, W., *Introduction to the Human Sciences*, London : Harvester Wheatsheaf (tr. R.J. Betanzps), 1988.

Dissanayake, W., "Communication, Knowledge and a Post-Industrial Society: The Need for Values-Centred Approach", in Christian Academy (ed.), *World Community in Post-Industrial Society*, Seoul: Wooseok Publishing Co., 1988.

Doordarshan 96, Audience Research Unit, Directorate General, Doordarshan, April 1996.

Erosov, B. and Yogendra Singh, *The Sociology of Culture*, Moscow: Progress Publishers, 1991.

Fox, R.G., *Kin, Clan, Raja and Rule: State Hinterland Relations in Preindustrial India*, Berkeley: University of California Press, 1971.

Gellner, E., *Postmodernism, Reason and Religion*, London: Routledge, 1992.

Geertz, C., *The Interpretation of Culture*, London: Hutchinson, 1975.

Hirst, P. and S. Khilnani, *Reinventing Democracy*, Oxford: Blackwell Publishers. 1996.

Kothari, Rajni, "Globalization and Revival of Tradition: Dual Attack on Model of Democratic Nation-Building", *Economic and Political Weekly*, March 25, 1995.

Krishna Kumar, T., "Management of Development in the Newly Emerging Global Economic Environment", *Economic and Political Weekly*, June 22, 1996.

Ludden, D., *Peasant History in South India*, Princeton, New Jersy: Princeton University Press, 1985.

Lyotard, J.F., *The Postmodern Condition: A Report on Knowledge*, translated by G. Bennigtomn and Massumi, Manchester: Manchester University Press, 1987.

Marriott, McKim, *Caste Ranking and Community Structure in Five Regions of India and Pakistan*, Poona: Deccan College, 1965.

Mencher, Joan P., *Agriculture and Social Structure in Tamilnadu: Past Origins, Present Transformations and Future Prospects*, Delhi: Allied, 1978.

Meenakshi, J.V., "How Important Are Changes in Taste? A State Level Analysis of Food Demand", *Economic and Political Weekly*, December 14, 1996.

Ministry of Information and Broadcasting, *Annual Report*, 1996-97, Government of India.

National Sample Survey, Government of India, 1972-73, 1973-74 1977-78, 1983 and 1987-88.

Oommen, T.K, "Social Movement and State Response: The Indian Situation", in A.M. Shah, B.S. Baviskar and E.A. Ramaswamy (eds.), *Social Structure and Change: Development and Ethnicity*, New Delhi: Sage Publications, 1977.

Ostor, Alos, *The Play of the Gods: Locality, Ideology, Structure and Time in the Festivals of a Bengali Town*, Chicago: Chicago University Press, 1980.

Peggy, Mohan, "Market Forces and Language in Global India", *Economic and Political Weekly*, April 22, 1995.

Pieterse, J.N., "Globalization and Culture: Three Paradigms", *Economic and Political Weekly*, June 8, 1996.

Radhakrishnan and Ravi C., "Effects of Growth, Relative Prices and Preferences on Food and Nutrition", *Indian Economic Review*, Special Number, 1992.

Schiller, H.I., "Current Views of Information and Media Power", in Christian Academy (ed.), *The World Community in Post-Industrial Society: Continuity and Change in Communication in Post-Industrial Society*, Seoul: Wooseok Publishing Co., 1988.

Singh, Archana, "Tourism", Review of 50 Years of Tourism Development in India, Mimeographed, 1997.

Singh, K.S., *People of India: An Introduction*, Calcutta: Anthropological Survey of India, 1992.

Singh, Yogendra, *Significance of Culture in the Understanding of Social Change in Contemporary India*, Presidential Address, New Delhi: Indian Sociological Society, 1994.

----, *Modernization of Indian Tradition*, New Delhi: Thompson Press, 1973.

----, "The Desired Form of Political Leadership and the New Economic Policy", Mimeographed, 1997.

Sivakumar, Chitra and S.S. Sivakumar, "Rural Change, Social History and Participant Observation", in A.M. Shah, B.S. Baviskar and E.A. Ramaswamy (eds.), *Social Structure and Change: Development and Ethnicity*, New Delhi: Sage Publications, 1997.

Srinivas, M.N., "Indian Anthropologists and Study of Indian Culture", *Economic and Political Weekly*, March 16, 1996.

States Reorganization Commission, *Report*, New Delhi: Publication Division, Government of India, 1955.

Stobes, Eric, *The Peasant and the Raj*, New Delhi: Vikas, 1978.

Stein, B., *Peasants, State and Society in Medieval South India*, Delhi: Oxford University Press, 1980.

Unnithan, T.K., Deva, Indra and Singh, Yogendra (eds.), *Towards a Sociology of Culture for India*, New Delhi: Prentice Hall of India, 1965.

Videsh Sanchar Nigam Ltd., *Annual Report*, 1995-96.

3

Is Globalization a Threat to Regional and Local Identities?

Globalization as a process signifies a unique development in human history. It gives a new dimension to the debate on modernization in contemporary societies. To what extent it signifies features which conform with 'post-modernity' remains to be established. This is particularly so in view of the fact that the questions of philosophical and epistemological nature, which are basic to the debate on post-modernity, are often avoided in most discussions on the processes of globalization. What has engaged the attention of analysts in the debates on globalization relates to its economic, technological, communicational, cultural or socio-political implications for the developing societies.

In the context of the developed nations, this debate no doubt relates to the post-industrial and post-modern phases of growth. Focus here is on the ontogenesis of these and philosophical and ethical issues that such societies encounter in their post-modern phase of development of science and technology, its linkages with economic, cultural, social and political institutions of society. By implication, most discussions on globalization---philosophical, ethical and epistemological---remain inward-looking. Only recently, particularly following the disintegration of the USSR, ethnic tensions on cultural and religious grounds have engaged the attention of analysts and thinkers. The hyper-competitive post-industrial economy of the developed countries generates fluctuating degrees of employment opportunities on the one hand, and on the other, its demographic necessity to import labour from less developed countries brings into their societies ethnic migrants in ever increasing numbers. This process eventually has resulted into sharpening of inter-cultural and inter-ethnic identities often leading to conflict and violence.

The cultural implications of such economic and demographic changes through globalization in the developed societies bear similarities with the nature of responses to the encounter with it in the developing societies. This similarity is not on account of the nature of problems faced as such, which no doubt have qualitative differences due to different levels of development in the two types of societies. The similarity remains because at this level the analysis of issues emerging from globalization tends to become more sociological than philosophical, which is the main concern today in the developing societies.

The issue of cultural identity assumes significance in the process of globalization as it impacts upon the social, cultural and economic life of people in different societies. Its pattern differs from one society to the other due to differences of historicity and the initial conditions which characterize their society and culture. It may also differ depending upon the nature of contact that the processes of globalization may have with the concerned societies or cultures; as to whether such contact is broad based covering a range of social, cultural and economic life of the people or it impacts upon a very selective aspect of their social, cultural, economic or other aspect of life. It is useful, therefore, to understand the process as well as the dimensions of globalization taking place in the developing societies.

DIMENSIONS OF GLOBALIZATION

Some 'universals of culture' common to all mankind have been a reality ever since the beginning of human history. This should not be confused with the sharing of cultures resulting from globalization. It had its basis in similarity of human nature at a certain level which led anthropologists to conclude that "man is like all other men" even though recognizing differences at other levels where they postulated "man is like some other men" and "man is like no other man". Indeed, this hierarchy or differentiation of levels in the constitution of human nature has defined both common and distinctive elements in culture. Identities are formed and tend to become meaningful at the subjective level of human nature and consciousness on the one hand, and on the other, through sharing cultural practices in common defined by the differences of territory, ecology, ethnicity and historical experiences of the people in societies. Similarly, the cultural reality of contemporary processes of globalization also did not exist in the past when inter-cultural contacts were established between societies either on the basis of imperial domination or colonization. The most important reasons for the distinctive historical phenomenon of globalization of cultures or the new challenges that it poses for the humanity can be traced to its unique technological base which has revolutionized the concept and quality of the systems of production, communication, social organization and the various processes of acculturation and symbolization in societies. In order to analyze the implications of globalization on regional and local cultures, it is necessary to examine the entirety of the processes covering its impact upon societies. This could be done first by understanding its various dimensions. Its main features are: (1) revolution in communication technology rendering global circulation of messages and symbols in the shortest time possible and proliferation and diversification of technological means for doing so; (2) circulation of financial capital on global scale searching for markets and economies of scale through international division of labour and structure of wages with introduction of high technology; (3) homogenization of consumer products and market processes both in the realms of commodities and cultural symbols, styles and behavioural patterns; (4) enlargement of the scope of electronic media through telephony, television, fax, e-mail, Internet, etc., putting enormous new pressures on traditional notions of sovereignty and autonomy of states or governments impacting deeply on political values, ideologies and movements; (5) very high and intense degree of circulation of manpower across countries and cultures creating articulate and culturally sensitive Diaspora of migrant population contributing to homogenization of cultures on the one hand, and to elevated sense of cultural identity and distinctiveness on the other. It is indeed valid as Arjun Appadurai (1966) argues that modern technologies of communication outcross the boundaries of real time and real space in social interactions. And, 'virtual communities' or groups may be possible, but it does not overcome the acuteness of crisis of cultural identities. Malaysia has almost opted out of the agenda of globalization reverting back to a closed economic model both in the economic and cultural sectors of their society. Indonesian intellectuals though still harbouring some hopes from globalization remain deeply concerned. But it may have to be recognized that such developments also do not eliminate emergence of a strong self-consciousness among people, both local and migrants, of their sense of cultural identity. This is because the process of globalization sets into motion several predictable as well as unanticipated problems in societies and cultures that encounter it in course of their social and economic developments. This issue assumes very sensitive proportion in most developing societies. This would be evident from the articulation of hopes and fears of intellectuals from these societies, particularly those from the East Asian countries and from South Asia.

The most widespread anxiety among these intellectuals pertains to the possibility of serious damage or loss of their cultural identity without commensurate benefits of economic and social developments through globalization of their economies. The recent economic turmoil in countries like Indonesia, Malaysia and Thailand and the kind of social, economic, political and ethnic crisis it has created in their societies, following the flight of international capital and financial collapse of the economy, has made both public and the intelligentsia extremely skeptical about the bounties of the reform paradigm of globalization. They tend to be extremely self-conscious about its fall-out in the economic, cultural and political-social fields. Loekman Soetrismo (1997) has expressed this feeling in his analysis of the consequences of globalization on social harmony, stability and diversity in the contemporary Indonesian society. He is suspicious of globalization in a form which acutely enlarges and intensifies the competition among unequal groups and societies without economic and social benefits of interdependence. The negative consequences of unequal competition not only create economic and social imbalances in relationships between the developed and the developing countries but also among the developing countries placed as they may be at different stages of development with variable advantages of competition. For instance, he mentions Indonesia has to compete for foreign investment with China, Vietnam and Bangladesh where wages are far lower and its higher wage regime works against its developmental interests. Globalization also does not contribute to cultural, social and economic integration of people in the society through equitable access to the fruits of developments available through globalization. Cultural conflicts or contradictions sharpen in society due to unlimited exposure of people to foreign cultural and entertainment packages beamed from television and other mass media. Soetrismo (1997: 6-7) further writes: "The spread of such culture worries those with more traditional values. For them globalization offers a menace towards their native culture. American or European culture is accused of subverting local culture. Reaction to this globalizing culture takes the form of revitalizing indigenous religion such as Islam. Islamic leaders see that globalization is spreading secularism among Moslems. Islamic leaders urge their followers to resist the influence of globalization by strengthening their Islamic identity. The word 'Islamic' becomes very popular among Moslems in Indonesia. There are Islamic psychology, Islamic economy, Islamic dress etc." (see also, Lodge, 1995).

Similar fears of globalization in the cultural field are reported from Vietnam----a former socialist country now moving towards globalization of economy. The cultural threats that globalization poses to this society are noted as: displacement of the traditional moral norms of society due to exposure to "dehumanizing and retrogressive cultural products" in the form of entertainment, consumerism, exposure to new style of life etc., leading to high incidence of crime and moral deviance such as prostitution, cult of money and loss of traditional humanistic values, disintegration of family life and age-old family values like care of the elderly and emotional bond among the members of family. This necessitates appropriate cultural policy to be implemented by the state along with economic reforms necessary to meet with the requirements of globalization. It is reflected in the resolution adopted at the 4th plenum of the Central Committee of the Communist Party of Vietnam, saying: "Development of the national culture must go along with the broadening of cultural exchanges with foreign countries, with absorbing the quintessence of human culture in order to enrich the national culture. Resolutely checking the infiltration of bad and noxious cultures and protecting the national culture" (Nguyen, 1997: 3). In terms of policy, this resolution has led to emphasis on reinforcement of family values, national cultural identity, reconstruction of educational system, planned development of culture and control by state on "the negative impact of the information explosion" in Vietnam.

The cultural policy of China is not much different from Vietnam. Being a much bigger country with greater geo-political aspirations and influence in the region, it, however, projects additional cultural nuances bordering to a kind of Asian cultural identity rather than entirely a national one. Not only has this emphasis on preservation of Asian cultural values been applauded by most other nations in the region, such as Indonesia, Malaysia, Singapore and Thailand etc., for reasons of preservation of cultural identity, but also by demonstrating a certain exclusiveness of political values and ideologies commensurate with their emphasis on the state control on the institutions of culture, rights of the citizens in making cultural choices and access to information. The plurality of political systems in the Asian region, however, necessitates that the paradigm of Asian culture is formulated in a manner that is broad enough to include many distinct cultural traditions. For instance, it is held that the "unity of heaven and man" (a theory that means man is an integral part of nature) in ancient Chinese philosophy, the thinking of "integration of Brahaman and Atman" in ancient India and the thinking of "integration of God and human" in Islamic philosophy are quite similar and thus have some common ideological connotations despite the plurality of religions, ethnic groups and nationalities in Asia. To quote:

> "The differences of cultures are fundamental reason for cultural diversification and also the active factor for its development. In Asia, there are some undeniable general features of the cultures of China, India and Arabian countries. And they will play a positive role in solving the series of current 'crises' in the world. There is no doubt that Asian people are proud of the glorious cultures created by their ancestors, but it is necessary that they should learn lessons from their backwardness in the past hundreds of years...The Chinese culture in the 21st century will carry forward and develop the good traditions, and fully reflect the spirit of the times. Moreover, at the same time that it is based itself on the motherland, it will orient towards the whole world" (Ru Xin, 1997:44).

The anxiety about the preservation of cultural identity in

the process of globalization seems to vary in terms of quality and degree depending upon the initial social and cultural structures of the concerned societies as well as their economic resilience. For instance, the reactions from South Korea and China to the impact of globalization on cultural identity seem to be more self-confident. The same could not, however, be said for the other Asian Pacific nations where the sensitivity to the threat to cultural identity in the process of globalization remains rather strong. The reactions also vary on account of the degree of social structural and cultural differentiation, and pluralities in the given society. Ethnically more homogeneous a society is, greater there is ease with which the leadership and people of that society get ready to cope up with the encounter with challenges of globalization. China and South Korea fall under this category. Such societies can also implement cultural and social policies to establish acceptable equilibrium of relationship of their local and regional cultures with cultural and economic forces released in the process of globalization. But, in the counties such as Indonesia, Malaysia and Thailand where ethnic and social structural pluralities and differentiation are strong, cultural and social anxieties on account of globalization remain very acute. The impact of globalization in these societies gets uneven results across inter-ethnic, inter-religious and inter-class boundaries. The resurgence of Islamic identity in Indonesia goes hand in hand with incipient and manifest expressions of hostility towards ethnic Chinese and Christians, and the uneven access to the fruits of globalization on account of educational, economic and social deprivations among the poorer Indonesians enlarges their anxiety and hostility towards globalization. It also renders them more vulnerable to ideologies----be they religious or cultural that almost demonise the notion of globalization.

CULTURAL RESPONSE FROM SOUTH ASIA

The countries from the South Asian region, such as India, Pakistan, Sri Lanka and Bangladesh, constitute a separate category where the experiences of history, geography, levels of economic development and social, cultural and ethnic differentiation and pluralities render their responses to the processes of globalization qualitatively different. Seen in a comparative perspective, globalization seems to have been received with much empathy and facility within Sri Lanka. Yet, the normative disapproval of consumerism in urban areas and the increasing economic disparities in society on account of uneven spread of advantages accruing to people through globalization remains high. Gunawardana (1997: 59) writes:

> "South Asian countries are now beginning to experience the uneven outcomes of globalization. Economic disparities are becoming more evident than before, thus opening the way of circumstances which, if unchecked, could eventually generate social instability and disharmony. The disjunctions evident in South Asian societies today are not confined to the sphere of economics and trade. It would appear that a new social ethic is emerging which has the potential to transform cultures by moulding them into a single global pattern of wasteful consumerism. But this homogenizing thrust of globalization is being resisted at different levels through appeals to culture, history, ethnicity, language, and similar vehicles of identity which are both national and subnational."

This process results not only in defining cultural identities through celebration of local cultural identities or growth of ever new forms of symbolization of nationalism or regionalism. It also encourages people to define their identities through religion or through its more extreme manifestation in the form of religious fundamentalism. We observe such tendencies in Pakistan, India and Bangladesh where an attempt is being made by a determined section of people and parties to make religion the basis of the national cultural ethos. This trend has led scholars like Huntington (1993) to postulate the likely future possibilities of "clash of civilizations" resulting into serious conflicts.

Huntington's thesis has been very widely contested by most Asian scholars. Questions have been raised about the implicit fallacies in his formulation of the notion of civilization entirely in religious terms as also about his neglect of the inter-civilizational elements of commonness such as between Islam and Christianity or between Confucianism, Hinduism and Islam. In this connection, the following observations of the President of the Chinese Academy of Social Sciences make eminent sense. He says:

> "Prof. Huntington of Harvard University published an article proposing a theory of the 'clash of civilizations'. He thinks that the main part of the international political struggle in the future will be caused by the clash among the main civilizations in the world, particularly, Confucianism might be united with the Islamic civilization, which will form a threat to the Christian civilization in the West. Then he makes a deduction that the 'clash of civilizations' will lead to a new World War. In the process of the economic globalization, there will be tendencies of mutual understanding and even mixture of main civilizations and national cultures, and, of course diversities and competitions as well. But it is both untenable academically and harmful politically to exaggerate this diversities and competitions to uncompromisable conflicts. With its ideological brand of the Cold War, the theory of the 'clash of civilizations' reflects some people's worry about the gradual weakening hegemony of the West" (Inaugural address on the 12th AASSREC Conference, Beijing, 1997: 6-7).

THE INDIAN SITUATION

We may now focus on the Indian situation. As we mentioned earlier, the quality and magnitude of the impact that globalization may have on the culture of a society would depend upon its initial social structural and cultural features. In this respect, the Indian social structure has historically inherited some very specific characteristics. The noteworthy amongst them are: caste-based plurality of communities; inter-structural autonomy at the normative level in the traditional society; and continuity of historical linkages despite the existence of enormous plurality of cultural patterns and styles at the local and regional levels. This is possible due to a broad civilizational unity based upon, techno-economic, political or administrative linkages, linkages through art and cultural styles and techniques articulated by both the elite and the folk traditions. It may be noted that through centuries the processes of "universalization and parochialization" have been going on in India, particularly in the realm of art and culture which established a meaningful relationship between the local cultures of specific tribes, castes or regions within an Indian cultural or civilizational matrix (Unnithan, Deva and Singh, 1965; Singh 1993: 149-167). There has existed a continued dialogue and interaction or even creative synthesis between the 'great traditions' or elite culture and that of the 'little tradition' or the culture of the folk or local communities.

The plurality of communities and cultural diversity in India is reflected in the recent survey by the Anthropological Survey of India in its Peoples of India (PoI) report. Communities have been defined in this survey "as in ethnography, which is marked by endogamy, occupation and perception" (Singh, 1992: 23). There are 4,635 communities in India, and sociologically they manifest themselves at various levels. Firstly, there are the very large categories of communities including castes and minorities, and secondly those that identify themselves through linguistic and cultural categories (such as Assamese, Bengali, Gujarati, Rajasthani, Tamil etc.). Some communities identify themselves through historical origin, e.g., Adi Dharma, Adi Andhra, Adi Karnataka, etc. But these are the communities falling in the first category which are preponderant.

The state-wise distribution of communities may give us some idea about the spread of the local cultures reflected in its diversity. The survey notes: "The communities are unevenly distributed in all states and union territories including Bay islands. By far the largest number of communities (above 350) are found in Andhra Pradesh and Tamilnadu. They vary from 250-350 in Uttar Pradesh, Bihar, Madhya Pradesh, Maharashtra, Orissa, Karnataka and Gujarat. The range varies from 150-250 in West Bengal, Rajasthan and Kerala. Arunachal Pradesh, Assam, Tripura, Jammu and Kashmir, Himachal Pradesh, Haryana and Panjab have communities ranging from 50-150. The number of communities drops to below 50 in Nagaland, Manipur, Mizoram, Meghalaya, Sikkim, Goa, Chandigarh and Bay islands" (Singh, 1992). The pattern of density and dispersal of communities as revealed by this survey may give us an idea about the scale of the plurality of local cultures and its regional differentiation. It is found that communities perceive their distribution at three levels: local or regional (within the existing boundary of state/ UT), the inter-regional (across the adjoining state boundaries) and the national, i.e., over a large part of the country. According to the data generated under the PoI project for 2,795 communities, 71.77 per cent identify themselves at the local level, i.e., within a state/UT, 24.26 per cent across the adjoining regions, and 3.97 per cent spread over a large part of the country (Singh, 1996: 5). Of the total (4,635) communities, 796 are distributed over the larger part of the country. More than one hundred communities perceive their dispersal internationally, and most of them interestingly come from Mizoram, Meghalaya Sikkim and Tripura.

The survey also has attempted to examine the relationship between community and religion and sharing of cultural traits by communities following different religions. All religious groups in India have plurality of communities: Muslims have 584 communities, Christians 339, Sikhs 130, Jains 100, Buddhists 93, Jews 7, Parsis 3 and tribals 411. This diversity of community base, together with regional dispersal within each religion, creates a variety of local cultural styles, normative practices and traditions. It outcrosses and is almost superposed on people's religious identities as it were. However, the diversity also co-exists with inter-community and inter-religious cultural linkages. This is found through the pattern of distribution of culture traits that the PoI survey has observed among communities and religious groups. It shows that "there is very high correlation of traits between the SCs (Scheduled Castes) and the STs (Scheduled Tribes), between the STs and Hindus, between Hindus and Sikhs, between Hindu and Muslims (which is very high indeed) and between Hindus and Jains. The high correlation between Hindus and Buddhists may also be explained in the same way. The fact that these communities interact across space or states is important" (Singh, 1992: 99).This commonality of culture traits is a result of historical depth, and social and cultural reciprocities and interactions among communities broadly sharing a common civilization of India.

The communities have their own local and regional cultural identity which is reflected through cultural 'markers', such as the design of the dress, style of turbans, tattoos, community flags and ornaments or ornamental decoration of the body. This variation has its basis in myths, legends and ritual practices, but it is also closely related to ecological and techno-economic level of development of the communities. The PoI survey concludes: "The picture of India that emerges, in spite of conflicts and contradictions, is also one of sharing of environment and ethos by communities and of their vibrant participation in political and economic processes and ritual roles. These facts explain why there has generally been a continuity and a sense of harmony prevails over a large part of the countryside in spite of conflicts that sometimes threaten to tear our social fabric apart and why return to normalcy is often quicker after every searing experience. India is also a land of migrants. There are very few communities which do not consider themselves to be migrants. Every community recalls its migration to the native habitat in its folklore and history. The whole of India is a *kshetra* (field) and an Indian is a migrant par excellence (Singh, 1992: 100).

Language has played a very important role in India in shaping not only the regional and local cultural identities but also its political and economic aspirations. Language policy formed an integral component of the ideology of freedom movement. Evidently, states were reorganized on linguistic principle soon after India attained independence. Language policy has remained an important element for national integration of India as a modern nation-state. Even today, several linguistic movements are going on based on regional, ethnic and political aspirations, and language provides a continued live issue in the perception of political and cultural identity of people at the regional and local levels. There are 325 languages spoken by various communities in different parts of India. But 33 languages are the major ones as they are spoken by 3,263 out of the total 6,435 communities. These languages are also common to the tribes, scheduled castes and other castes reflecting the larger extent of linguistic sharing. Most of these languages and also the other ones which have significant speech community are recognized by the state for media broadcast, medium of teaching and also for official uses. Being a sensitive issue not only of identity but also politics in a democratic set-up languages have constituted in India a very significant marker of local and regional aspirations and states policy of reconciliation and continued accommodation. Nevertheless, the increased level of inter-regional and inter-state interaction among people during the past fifty years, either due to economic factors such as migration for employment or education or shared media exposure through television, radio, films and magazines or newspapers etc., has led to a very high degree of growth in bilingualism and creolization of the spoken languages. The PoI survey reveals that bilingualism was 13.4 per cent on a conservative estimate in 1971; this reached the level of 64.2 per cent in 1991. About 58.91 per cent communities listed in the Constitution of India are now bilingual. The creolization of linguistic usages is a result of increased interaction between tribal and non-tribal population, says the survey of PoI (Singh, 1992).

Yet, another significant feature of the traditional Indian society that influences the impact of globalization processes on local, regional and national cultures of India is the special role that caste and its associated normative structures have played in enabling the society to maintain inter-structural autonomy of a very significant level with ability to absorb and adapt to the cultural contacts from outside. This characteristic of the traditional Indian society reflected itself in the principle of autonomy between the political authority and the priestly or moral authority. Those who had control over *artha* or the institutions of power and wealth did not have the legitimacy to pronounce judgement on cultural, moral and religious issues. Similarly, "caste panchayats" or councils played a very major role in the governance of matters related to the cultural, social and economic life of the community. These panchayats, which usually comprised caste members belonging to several villages with nucleus in each village also played the role of judicial and administrative authority in all matters concerning the members of a caste and their relationship with other castes. However, in most other matters of judicial and administrative authority, the village council or administrative institutions of state performed the functions of enforcement of rules, regulations and customs. This autonomy in matters of governance at the levels of caste and village or in the urban centres that of various caste-guilds etc., provided enormous structural and cultural resilience to the local communities to maintain their autonomy and also to regulate their responses to cultural and social contacts with other cultures.

This is amply reflected in the selective, graduated and adaptive patterns of responses that Indian society and culture have demonstrated in its contacts with the outside cultural traditions through centuries. The contact with the western civilization, unique in its character due to its colonial form anchored on industrial revolution, was the first encounter which had an overwhelming influence for two reasons: the British colonizers remained alien in India as a matter of policy, and secondly, the institutional and cultural innovations they introduced in the society had an enduring appeal to the Indian elite as a paradigm of modernization. The debate which followed in this historical contact with the West had also the making of a challenge. It led to introspection on matters of cultural identity, reform and renaissance. The entire gamut of the evolution of a national ideology on this issue is contained in the history of the Indian national movement and the policies pursued following independence.

The policies to bring about radical social, economic and cultural or ideological changes in the society carried out with much fervour since independence have not been able to erode the overwhelming influence of caste, local communities and regional cultural identities even though emphasis remained on centralized planning and the relevance of decentralization and self-rule was not fully recognized in the early years of the planning process. This planned effort was based on the ideology which did not recognize caste and religion as building blocks in the archaeology of a secular democratic nation-state. At the operative level of social, economic and cultural processes of change, however, these institutions have manifested themselves during the past fifty years with new vigour. Of course, their adaptive responses to policies of modernization or globalization have now assumed an entirely new ideological flavour.

GLOBALIZATION AND CULTURAL IDENTITY

Cultural identities are shaped by a complex set of factors which are associated with the processes of evolution of cultural practices and beliefs of a people in course of their historical experiences. Ecological setting, basic economic institutions and work related to it, the family structure and child rearing processes, stories, myths and legends along with history, constitute some of the elements which give identity to a culture as it manifests itself through symbolic expressions in material artifacts, expressive behaviour, belief systems, language, literature, etc. The members belonging to a community internalize this identity both consciously as ideologies (as identity is continually rationalized) and also unconsciously in the process of the formation of their "basic personality structure". For this reason, a distinction can always be made between the conscious or manifest and unconscious or latent levels of cultural identities. All adaptive responses towards outside culture, therefore, even in the best of motivational situation, involve anxiety and have to go through a process of nationalization (justification through new ideology) and eventually through internalization of new cultural values in the personality system. Cultural identities, therefore, constitute a dynamic process which are ever responsive to changes in the historical, social, economic and techno-ecological situations encountered by a community. Such identities, no doubt, have a core which is most enduring and resists radical changes in its structure. Such changes usually begin at the periphery of the structure of cultural identity and take a very long time indeed, in altering the core of the cultural identity of a people. The local, regional and national levels of manifestation of cultural identities from a sociological perspective only represent different stages of rationalization and abstraction of the structure of such identities.

Globalization process in this respect constitutes a very special kind of manifestation of inter-cultural encounters and reciprocities. It is different in many ways from the process of westernization which largely in the colonial setting of the past implied cultural encounters between a dominant techno-economic power from abroad and its subject people. Even though such perceptions (specially after the economic crisis faced by the Asia-Pacific nations) are not quite irrelevant in the eyes of many Third World citizens even in the case of globalization process, it is generally recognized that the two processes are historically and qualitatively different. Globalization with the possible exception of the circulation and transactions of capital through the international agencies, such as the IMF and the World Bank etc., or through the corporate banking sectors or consortia, has a more reciprocal and interactive dimension. The banking and financial capital which in the process of globalization is supposed to flow into the investment channels of the developing nations in search of profitable markets has not proved to be free from narrow and short-sighted profit-seeking orientation even of the speculative nature. This has led to a very widespread thinking among the Third World governments and intelligentsia that like the process of the colonial westernization of the past, globalization too is yet another variant of the process of the western economic, technological and cultural domination. Few nations in the world today are, however, prepared to totally sever their relationship with globalization process. No doubt, a widely accepted viewpoint now prevails that new institutional mechanism is necessary to regulate the speculative and unscrupulous capital and banking operations by the private banks (often with complicity of the local political leadership) as also there is need for the reorientation of the policies of the international capital and banking institutions such as the IMF and the World Bank in order to overcome these serious flaws in the system.

Money and market are the overarching factors through which all other major elements in the globalization process gain momentum. The other most important element in this process is the revolutionary changes in the technology of communication and travel which for the first time in human history has brought inter-cultural interactions among people to a level which a few decades ago was beyond human imagination. This has been made possible through television, Internet, e-mail, fax and other forms of communication through electronic media. The satellite communication has revolutionized the context of communication and its reach to people strengthening both market and dimensions of the inter-cultural contacts among diverse settings of culture and civilization. However, its impact, as we have noted earlier, is not uniform, and differs from level to level of cultural contact and the context in which globalization process takes place.

IMPACT ON LOCAL, REGIONAL AND NATIONAL CULTURES

We may evaluate the impact of globalization on local, regional and national cultures of India in the context of the issues mentioned above. From the portrayal of the social structural characteristics of Indian society and its historicity, it should be evident that both local cultures and its regional representations have enjoyed a great deal of autonomy. But this autonomy did not imply insulation of these cultures from the civilization of India. Strong linkages existed and reciprocal interactions in terms of inclusion and exclusion of culture traits, styles and forms continually took place at all the three levels of the cultural traditions. Studies of folk culture and its patterns of distribution in various regions have demonstrated strong similarities in thematic, stylistic and ritualistic expressions in the form of songs, ceremonies, rituals and conventions. This has only been confirmed by the survey conducted by the PoI recently. Its findings substantiate the fact that culture traits are not only shared in common between regions but also among diverse communities and religious groups in India.

The concept of locality and local culture in India cannot be separated from the notions of caste, tribe, ethnic groups or communities which are territorially located. The nature of territory, its ecology, economy and local customs and traditions endowed the cultural practices of these people with local flavour. The cultural identity of local communities was based upon occupational specialization, its related rituals and belief systems and in many cases on ritual or religious symbolization of material products, e.g., works of art, animal and food products, institutions dealing with social and cultural life of the local community, especially women, children and precious community resources. One very important institution which traditionally dealt with such matters was the panchayat of the concerned caste or tribe. Its significance extended from the territorial setting of a village or settlement to a region. In this sense, the notions of locality and region as sociological categories have interrelated significance operating at different levels of demand. The tribal communities or ethnic groups had in addition many specialized institutions to deal with the functions of socialization and education of younger members, celebration of rituals and ceremonies specific to the tribe or the ethnic group.

Both caste and tribe have local existence in the sense that they are settled in the territorial boundary of a village. Generally, one may find three types of such settlements: (i) multi-caste villages without tribal population, (ii) villages having many caste groups with some population of the tribes, and (iii) villages populated by tribes exclusively. Within the village, with the exception of castes having a single family such as the many artisan castes, each caste group has maintained its own specific culture and local traditions. In the regional setting, the role of the caste panchayat assumed significance because it constituted the confederation of individual caste spread over a region. Studies of the spatial distribution of a single caste in many regions of India have revealed that hardly any caste group in India has a territorial spread beyond 200 miles. Most of them exist within a radius of about 50 miles only, and beyond this distance their meaningfulness ceases to exist except in terms of the notion of *varna* which is an abstract model. Caste is, therefore, a regional social institution. So is the tribe. Yet, they are also contributors to local cultures all over the country (Singh, 1973).

The question logically arises: what is the difference between the local and regional culture in India? Sociologically, the local culture exists in a specific context of a village or settlement (with the exception of the nomadic groups). Its cultural space is defined by the sacred geography, temples, ponds, seats of gods and spirits, the distribution of totemic plants and animals and the burial or cremation sites etc. The physical and ecological landscape is endowed with memories of history, legend and myth. Many rituals and ceremonies, both related to calendar and lifecycle, have association with places and objects which are locally existent and carry strong emotional and cultural meaning for the people. Folk songs and dances tend to have allusive relationship with such objects and events which renders them locally meaningful. Sometimes local groups and families specialize in crafting works of art or have special styles in preparation of the ritual objects which go into the making of the local culture. And local castes, tribes or communities take pride in their achievement. Such endeavours also become subject of regional competition, aspiration and search for excellence. Such local cultural identity does not, however, exist in total isolation from the regional or national cultural identity.

The regional culture is based on ingredients which, despite sharing common attributes with the local cultures, have their focus upon cultural traits of much wider following and commitment. Historically, language has formed an important factor in India around which regional cultural identity has been articulated. We have mentioned how soon after independence states in India were reorganized on linguistic basis in order to satisfy people's regional cultural aspirations. Even now demands from various regional and ethnic groups in the country are still going on, e.g., demand from the Urdu-speaking Muslim population for recognition of Urdu language with fuller state support and its promotion to safeguard the cultural identity of the community. Similar demands are being articulated by the ethnic Gorkhas in the state of West Bengal, the Santhal tribe of Bihar, and several other tribes in many parts of the country. In addition to language, the regional cultural identities are also anchored to traditions of various social and cultural movements specific to the region, their fairs and festivals, culinary culture, dress and style of living, contributions to art, literature and knowledge, heroic or legendary contributions from eminent personalities in their history or their mythic construction of the past energizing their self-consciousness as a people of cultural distinction.

Cultural identities, whether local or regional, are activated not entirely because of the cultural self-consciousness endogenous to peculiar configuration of cultural style or historical achievements of the concerned communities. Many exogenous factors have assumed a great deal of relevance in making communities and ethnic groups acutely aware of their cultural identity. Some of the more important factors in this context are: the feeling of relative deprivation in economic, social and educational fields in comparison with other regional communities, their perception of the role of the market in preserving their autonomy and control over their products both cultural and material, the degree of their confidence in being able to utilize institutions of state and their own voluntary efforts for their social, cultural and economic mobility and empowerment and finally, their perception of the possible threat to their cultural identity from sources outside their own culture tradition.

The movements related to the issues of cultural identity of various communities and ethnic group, whether in the local or the regional context, fully demonstrate their sustained organizational and cultural mobilization to articulate their demands for greater share in education, civil and professional services, economic and social empowerment and access to resources to live a life of quality and dignity comparable with better off sections of society. The search for cultural identity, therefore, cannot be totally separated from the political processes in which the people are involved. In a democratic society, this process assumes added significance. This is reflected in the proliferation of various caste-based associations, tribal associations and associations of minorities and ethnic groups during the past fifty years. The issue of positive discrimination in government services for the members of the backward classes, the demand for creation of new states based on the ethnic composition of regional population, etc., are indicators of such developments. The demand for positive discrimination in government services now by religious minorities is gaining new momentum. All these processes tend to intensify the sense of identity and solidarity among the local and regional communities. As the process of democratization takes more roots in the country there is increasing self-awareness among people about their degree of relative deprivation and consequently identities are not only sharpening with vigour. Identities are also being continually constructed. Cultural symbols are important in such processes of identity constructions. This is exemplified by the emphasis on construction of distinct identity by the Dalits in relation to the Hindus or by several tribes in contrast with other ethnic and religious groups in various parts of the country. Studies show that castes, tribes and ethnic groups are increasingly becoming self-conscious about their own past, and there is interest in new explorations of myths and legends of the past among several castes and tribes. For example, *jati puranas* existed in cases of many caste groups in most parts of the country, but they were not made use of as now. Local communities now increasingly relish the celebration of their identity in distinction with other groups in a region or at the national level.

How does globalization process affect cultural identities of local and regional groups given the sociological processes discussed above? What kind of threat do these local and regional cultures perceive or encounter in reality as globalization in the fields of economy, communication, travel and tourism, migration and market interaction gains new momentum? What is the relationship between ever new inspirations of the local and regional groups to construct identities in cultural, social and political realms and the perceptions of threat to their cultural identity on account of globalizaton? How extensive and intense is the perception of this threat to the local and regional cultures, and how does it manifest itself through social and cultural movements or through pressure on the state to regulate cultural policies?

To deal with these questions, it is necessary to place them into objective historical and sociological settings. At the national level, the perception of threat to cultural identity of India as a nation or as a civilization has been of a long standing. It was well articulated by national leaders during the national movement, and despite the colonial relationship of India with the West, leaders like M.K. Gandhi and Jawaharlal Nehru did not favour a cultural policy of isolationism. The Constitution that free India chose to adopt as a secular democratic nation reflects this in a large measure; the cultural policy of the state has always been oriented towards preserving the best part of the Indian culture and civilization through institutional support, educational policies and protection of the cultural heritage of the tribes, minorities and communities located at the periphery of the mainstream culture of India. Combined with the economic, social and political reforms, envisaged and implemented during the past fifty years, this ideological response of India to the West went into the making of its modernization process. These factors had exposed the local and regional cultures to the forces of industrialization, urbanization, expansion of markets and professional and technological entrepreneurship as never before. Even though, a policy of import substitution in economic planning had delimited the scope of contact with the processes of globalization, the local and regional cultures did, nevertheless, have to go through radical changes in orientation in their cultural structures, practices and values in this process which demanded new cultural responses to the emergent changes in economy, polity and patterns of social mobility in society.

Hence, local and regional cultures in India do not encounter the exposure to globalization processes (following the introduction of new economic policies since 1991) with any acute sense of surprise. The impact of the pre-globalization economic and social policies had itself been such that local and regional cultures were forced to restructure their cultural identities. In the villages, the rise of the new middle class of dominant peasant castes triggered off a process of urban-ward migration and politicization that has contributed to the breakdown in the community values in villages, has made it extremely faction ridden. The relationships of cooperation and reciprocity among castes in a village, which in the past was the basis of a common cultural identity or contributed to collective efforts in the celebration of traditional fairs, festivals and major cultural events etc., has now become rare if it has not totally disappeared. Many such fairs and festivals are increasingly being commercialized and market impulses are fast encroaching upon the cultural landscape of Indian villages. Many cultural features which were once attributed to the urban cultural styles are now frequently observed to have a place in the local culture of a rural community. Cultural activities in rural areas which earlier were based on the participation of the entire village or local community have now increasingly become associative and entrepreneurial. Although, they are now being more efficiently organized but at the same time have lost the age-old participatory character. This has been happening to local cultures in most parts of the country even before the globalization process gained policy support and brought in possibilities of new dimensions of inter-cultural contacts through new modes of communication and market openings.

This simply highlights the fact that local and regional cultures had been exposed to destabilizing processes even before the onset of the globalization process. Hence, the significance of the perception of threat to their cultural identity in the process of globalization only represents the enlargement of the scale and the intensity of the interactive relationship rather than a totally unexpected experience. On the one hand, globalization extends the scope of commercialization of culture, and on the other, it also threatens the identity of local cultures by appropriating culture from people's rhythm of life to the market situation. It had its origin before the globalization process began, but its pace now is much more intense and its reach through global market very extensive indeed. Particularly affected in this process are the castes or communities engaged in production of arts and crafts, a large part of the household ritual activities in which women engage themselves, their sacred paintings and graphics or other sacred objects of artistic value. Due to the intrusion of market ethos, such objects are being traded as prized commodities. But, in this process, their meaning and significance is torn out of context which is often perceived as a threat to local and regional cultural identity. Nevertheless, such developments also have their compensatory values. Globalization of market for such ritual-artistic objects also provides much needed support to the local artisans—both men and women—engaged in the production of ritual objects of artistic value for which the demands in the local community had already suffered as a result of decline in patronage due to the disintegration of the traditional community ethos resulting from the impact of industrialization, urbanization and migration outside the local or regional habitat. It is an irony though, that despite such advantages accruing to groups engaged in the production of traditional art objects etc., the incorporation of such goods in the market network through globalization is looked at with nostalgic disapproval by the members belonging to the local culture. Often it is perceived as no less than a threat to the local or regional cultural identity.

An important consequence of globalization can be witnessed in the revolution in the electronic media of communication and entertainment, e.g., television, Internet, multimedia, satellite channels, etc. These have truly globalized the means for sharing cultural experiences and interactions. Probably, an unintended consequence of the globalization is that it also strengthens local and regional cultural identities. The scope of the electronic communication and entertainment media, though expanding rapidly, still remains limited due to continuing poverty, illiteracy and backwardness of about 40 per cent of the population. Nevertheless, radio and television have increased their reach to people in a phenomenal degree during the past few decades.

The radio listening has become a mass-based medium of information and entertainment. It covers 94.5 per cent of population. In 1997, there were about 187 radio stations and 297 operational transmitters. Moreover, the radio transmission policy, like any other media policy, has been acutely sensitive to the protection of cultural interest and aspirations of local and regional cultures. Each state and within each state for different linguistic and cultural groups adequate time slots have been provided both on radio broadcasting and television. Broadcasts and telecasts are done in several regional languages and cater to the interests of minorities, tribal groups and weaker sections of society. The television coverage is comparatively limited, as yet only about 50-60 per cent of population view programmes. But following the launch of India's satellites of the INSAT series and coming of the foreign media corporations in this field, multichannel viewing has become most common. This medium, too, takes the interests of the regional cultures into account in the telecast policy.

Films continue to occupy a place of pre-eminence as a medium of entertainment. In 1996 alone 683 films were produced in 23 languages, which included even films in the languages of smaller ethnic groups and minorities, e.g., Urdu, Manipuri, Garhwali and Rajasthani etc. Other channels of communication and entertainment such as computers, Internet, multimedia and cellular phones, etc., are still in limited use. There are, at present, only 200,000 Internet subscribers in the country. But considering the fact that in 1995, there were only 10,000 subscribers, the pace of expansion is indeed fast, and in many regions in India, particularly more developed states of western and southern parts, the expansion is very fast indeed. The policy of ending the monopoly of the state in the telecommunication sector is extending the reach of telephones, cellular phones, public call offices with a very fast pace. Apart from having a positive impact on industries and agriculture, it has the potential of adding new dimensions to local and cultural identities.

How are the local and regional cultures affected by such changes in the communication technology? Does it weaken or strengthen their cultural identities? The processes of growth in this area so far manifests complex results. Its impact on the local economy, commerce, banking, market (in agricultural, industrial and cultural products etc.) and information services etc., is certainly going to empower the regional and local entrepreneurs as never before. On local and regional cultures it may have both positive and negative impacts given the specificity of circumstances. As we have already discussed, the penetration of external market and capitalist interests may threaten local or regional cultures by new modes of appropriation and erosion of traditional cultural values. This may indeed be perceived as threat. But improvement and enlargement of the reach of communication may provide means to people to strengthen cultural identities through intensification of contacts, visual and auditory across the limits of space and time, which may contribute not only to the strengthening of existing cultural identities but also in giving these identities entirely new orientations. The existence of 'virtual communities' in addition to the real time communities or local groups through the new communication technology may be a matter of the future, but the immediate result of changes in the telecommunication sector does not rule out the possibilities of new empowerment of local and regional cultural identities.

It is to be noted that the social structural basis of the local culture though anchored into the boundaries of territory, caste, tribe and ethnicity extends also to the social and cultural structure of a region. Even though language may constitute a distinctive demarcation by which regional identities may be easily denoted or constructed, it does not exhaust all the social and cultural features which may go into making of a region. The PoI survey has been able to demarcate 91 cultural regions in India on the basis of the distribution of the culture traits. The factors which give a region a separate identity according to this study are: "distinct language/ dialect, territorial identity, cultural variations and varying levels of economic growth" (Singh, 1992: 53). The notion of territory is itself grounded into the dynamic relationship that its ecology, agro-industrial potential, natural resources and advantages of location in political and cultural sense endow it with a definitive identity. In addition, sub-regional processes continue to emerge as a result of uneven access to resources, levels of development and interest-group mobilization of people within a region. To accord legitimacy to such movements new cultural constructions of sub-regional identities are an ongoing process. The political demands for creation of new states or recognition of regional dialects as official language, demands for greater autonomy for administration in a sub-regional setting within the states etc., are instances of the dynamics of the continual processes of new identity formation and its rationalization through culture, economy, ecology, history and polity.

The processes of globalization which involve tremendous exposure of local, sub-regional and regional social entities to the forces of market and finance on the one hand, and on the other access to revolutionary means of communication and media, not only influence but also energize latent aspirations of these groups to re-invigorate and re-fashion their cultural identities. In this sense, the globalization process, instead of being a threat to such identities, has become a means for their construction.

CULTURAL HOMOGENIZATION VERSUS CULTURAL IDENTITY

No doubt, globalization leads to homogenization of cultures in some significant aspects throughout the world. Unlike the colonial cultural contact that several developing countries had with the West, and which was largely characterized by a relationship of domination rather than reciprocity, globalization involves interdependency, reciprocity and exchange of mutual skills and resources in a large measure. It does not, however, imply that the nature of reciprocity in global relationships is entirely equilateral; the inequalities based on capital, technological prowess and human resources remain. These factors create negative perceptions about globalization process in the mind of people and intelligentsia, particularly from the developing countries, about the motivation of the rich nations and of their financial and political institutions about the authenticity of the nature of interdependence in such relationships. The economic crisis faced recently by the nations of the Asia-Pacific region illustrates this fact. This perception, as also the reality of asymmetry in the financial and market levels in the globalization process, has endowed it with double significance: on the one hand, globalization contributes to homogenization of many cultural attributes across the globe, on the other, it generates suspicions and anxieties about the meaning and significance of such relationships. The result is that homogenization of cultures takes place in several aspects of cultural life of the people due to globalization, but this process also accelerates the growth of cultural self-consciousness and cultural identities.

It may be noted, however, that in India both homogenization of cultural traits as well as formation of local and regional or even sub-regional cultural identities began with the process of economic, political and cultural-educational modernization since the beginning of independence. This contributed to the growth of internal market, rise of the rural and urban middle classes, growth in the productivity of agriculture, horticulture, milk production and fisheries etc. Significant levels of growth in urbanization, industrialization and human resources in science, technology and professions were also achieved. This growth, however, was not even in all the states or regions of the country, and it has caused massive internal migration of labour; also the educated and professional manpower has been migrating to regions where they found better job opportunity. The incremental rate of growth in the number of middle classes which is now estimated to be around 300 million, has extended the scope for both status mobility and spatial mobility within and outside the country. Thus, not only the scope of market is substantially enlarged but significant purchasing power has been created which has impacted on the living styles and consumption patterns of a large number of people. Expansion of the telecommunication networks, people's additional exposure to entertainment and information through mass media, particularly television and cinema, have brought about changes in people's taste and have also increased the incidence of acceptability of inter-regional and international items in areas of food, beverages, dress patterns and many other culture traits in the style of living.

The economic and communication policies, which started in 1991 and set the basis for globalization process, have only augmented the pace and intensity of such changes. Studies reveal a very significant level of homogenization of dress patterns among the educated and semi-literate population of India across the country. The change is particularly visible in cases of the younger generation. The women's wear *salvar-kamiz*, for instance, is now a popular dress among most younger women throughout the country. Traditionally, it was confined to northern India and Panjab. But, now, it is particularly noticeable in the south, which has traditionally been more conservative. The use of synthetic materials in dress has also become common in the country. So are acceptability or even high prestige accorded to foreign designer dresses. Such dresses or their imitations are common wear now countrywide. Indian dress designers, who have entered the market in a big way, are not only encouraging both ethnicity and indigenous traditions in dress and cosmetics but also bringing about a fusion of styles and motifs in a broad cosmopolitan inter-cultural perspective. The use of modern cosmetics, generally of western origin, has become very fashionable these days and also commands a big market. Yet, the ethnic challenges to this industry based on folk and classical Indian medicinal tradition in cosmetics is also growing, and in the usual style of globalization has entered the international market in a big way.

What is true in the area of dress, is also happening in consumption patterns. Since the past few decades, the consumption of milk, eggs, fruits, fish, meat, etc., has gone up considerably following the phenomenal increase in their production. India, today, is world's biggest producer of milk in terms of gross production. During the past few decades, there has been a near revolution in the country in the production of fruits, expansion of fisheries, and poultry farming. The rise in the number of the new middle classes has provided these commodities a responsive and expanded market. Consumption of eggs has become so widespread that it can be seen being hawked all over the country and its acceptability has increased manifold. Non-vegetarianism is also increasing fast. The National Sample Surveys conducted in the country illustrate the incidence of radical changes in people's food habits; people are changing from the older pattern of heavily cereal based diet to a diet rich in protein content and fruits and vegetables. This change is not confined to any particular region although its intensity may vary. People are fast taking to this change in their consumption pattern even in the less developed regions of the country.

The rise in the number of the urban middle class population, particularly the working women, is fast bringing about radical changes in the food and beverages market in the country. Food processing and packaging is on the increase. The market for such food is increasing not only for the foreign items which still remain regulated, but more importantly, for the traditional Indian food items. The Indian Diaspora, whose number is increasing fast, provides rich market for it, and the same is slowly moving towards a global market. We, therefore, witness both tendencies towards globalization and ethnicization of the consumption pattern in India which no doubt constitutes a very significant facet of cultural identity in any society (Singh, 1997). Within India, the trend to consume and patronize food items of other regions and its culinary practises by members not belonging to that region is now growing fast due to increased inter-regional migration. Similarly, in the fields of many ritual and religious observations too, inter-regional homogenization seems to be in evidence. For instance, Durga Pooja (the worship of the icon of goddess Durga) which a few decades ago was confined to West Bengal, Orissa and Assam, has now spread to entire Bihar and Uttar Pradesh, besides being patronized in most cities throughout the country where ethnic groups from these regions have migrated. One witnesses a substantial degree of enhancement among local, regional and other ethnic or religious groups about the feeling that their cultural styles and forms should have an all-India or even global reach. Globalization process in some respects, therefore, not only encourages and leads to homogenization of local and regional cultures but also creates the urge among the local and regional cultures to acquire a global reach in celebration of its identities.

This pattern is not confined only to rituals, consumption styles or other overt aspects of culture. More importantly, it shapes the cultural identity of people across various regions and localities in India through the cultural values and ideologies they cherish most in their heart and mind. Their exposure to global cultural values and practises, their participation in institutional and organizational structures that globalization makes imperative, and their adoption of values and behaviours commensurate with such activities do not seem to bring about any meaningful extent of erosion of their cultural identities. It has been noticed that even those Indians who are working in the American or British software companies where they have to familiarize themselves with not only the new language needed for their work, but also its 'mind-set', do remain rooted to their own cultural identity and its ethos. Some form of 'cultural fusion', no doubt, takes place. To quote:

> "Cultural fusion is another common feature. Since these companies are outposts of American or British firms and adhere to their standards, they must master not only the unfamiliar terms but also the mind-set behind them. At Selectronic, a six-month training course in American medical terminology is supplemented with group viewing of Chicago Hope and ER accompanied by take away pizza. Yet, in some ways the atmosphere remains resolutely Indian. These data-workers are not rootless part-timers, as their American equivalents might be. Many expect their employers to treat them like family members, providing transport to and from work, company cricket games and jobs for life" (*The Economist*, 1999:63).

Not only the working population in modern corporate setting but also the school and college going younger generation in India has shown enough evidence, as many recent surveys and studies reveal, that despite its exposure to the Internet, pop culture and cell-phone and other cultural trappings of the emerging global cultural ethos, its basic cultural identities remain rooted into the Indian cultural moorings such as family values, care of parents, appreciation of traditional cultural forms and styles of music, art, painting and architecture. Even at the level of popular culture of music, dance, dramatics and cinema etc., the new trend is that of fusion of traditional folk classical Indian styles and forms of music, dances and its instrumental accompaniments with those from western and other global forms and styles. The popular culture, which thrives on the cultural globalization process and is itself deeply enmeshed with its market, capital and commodity ethos is not able to survive in India without drawing rather heavily from its folk, ethnic and other indigenous cultural traditions (Singh, 1997). This process of adaptation and fusion of cultural traits drawn from a variety of traditions of India by the emergent popular culture, does pose a threat to the indigenous local, regional or ethnic identity of cultural traditions in so far as it abstracts culture from people's rhythm of life and its natural expressiveness or vitality, and converts it by its new packaging into a commodity. In this process, community identity traditionally rooted in the kinship structure, caste and clan, principles of hierarchy and reciprocities, deeply embedded in community life are metamorphosed into a faceless 'audience' celebrated by the power of mass media. But as I have argued, these processes of change cannot be blamed entirely on globalization policy, which in our country has a history of less than a decade. This travail is rather germane in the very paradigm of modernization which we along with the rest of humanity wilfully celebrate.

SUMMING UP

The process of globalization does usher in many technological, economic, ecological and social changes in society which affect the traditional cultural styles, forms and ideologies. The extent to which it may constitute a threat to local and regional cultural identities in India depends largely on the manner in which globalization is perceived by the people concerned. Where it hurts the vital economic interests of the farmers, traders, industrial and agricultural workers, etc., its threat perception remains rather strong. There is even social mobilization to withhold rather than withstand the encounter with globalization. In the realm of culture, the threat that local and regional cultures perceive from globalization is strongly qualified. Several factors seem to influence and qualify its impact. In the first instance, globalization is only in its nascent phase, and India still has about 70 per cent of population dependent on agriculture. The traditional community ethos of the village has been eroded by politicization of people but the ties of caste, family, religion and rituals remain strong. The plurality of these structures endows local and regional cultures, which are anchored to them, a strong sense of resilience. It substantially subdues the threat perception. Globalization, in fact, is perceived as a friendly process by traditional local artisans, craftsmen and artists, etc., because they find in it a scope for economic empowerment and social mobility. Globalization also encourages them, linked as it is to the international market and capital, to innovate upon their ethnic styles, forms and materials in the cultural products. It adds new dimensions to their sense of cultural identity instead of leading to its erosion.

In the realm of the non-material culture, values, beliefs, rituals and religious practises, it is observed that globalization only enhances the consciousness of cultural identity. This process is aided by increase in cultural self-consciousness in the local, regional, ethnic and migrant communities as they come into contact with other cultures. Communication media are made use of to extend the scope of coverage of the cultural celebrations and rituals across local, regional or even national boundaries. The ethnic Diaspora only reinforces this urge for celebration of one's cultural identity. It is also strengthened by the rising section of the new middle classes and the series of cultural and social movements which today they lead in the country with a focus upon local and regional cultural identities as a part of their political, economic and cultural agenda.

References

Appadurai, Arjun, *Modernity at Large: Cultural Dimensions of Globalization*, Minneapolis: University of Minnesota Press, 1996.

Gunawardana, A.J., "Local Habitation and a Name", paper presented on "Asian Perspectives on Social Harmony, Social Stability and Diversity in Globalizing Societies", at the 12th AASSREC Conference, Beijing, 1997.

Huntington, Samuel P., "The Clash of Civilizations", *Foreign Affairs*,

Summer, 1993.

Lodge, C. George, *Managing Globalization in the Age of Independence*, Pfeiffer and Co., 1995.

Nguyuen, Huu Thuy, "Globalisation versus Preservation and Elevation of the National Cultural Identity", paper presented at the 12th AASSREC Conference, Beijing, 1997.

Ru Xin, "Economic Globalization and Asian Culture", paper presented at the 12th AASSREC Conference, Beijing, 1997.

----, "Economic Globalization and Asian Culture", Abstract: Proceedings of the XII AASSREC Conference, Beijing, 1997.

Singh, K.S., *People of India: An Introduction*, Calcutta, Anthropological Survey of India, 1992.

----, Identity, Ecology, *Social Organization, Linkages and Development Process: A Quantitative Profile,* Volume VII, New Delhi: OUP, 1996.

Singh, Yogendra, *Modernization of Indian Tradition*, New Delhi: Thompson Press, 1973.

----, "Globalization and Local Cultures: Issues and Perspectives in India", paper presented at 12th AASSREC Conference, Beijing, 1997.

Soetrismo, Loekman, "Social Harmony, Stability and Diversity in Globalizing Societies", paper presented at the AASSREC Conference, Beijing, 1997.

Unnithan, T.K., Deva, Indra and Singh, Yogendra (eds.), *Towards a Sociology of Culture in India*, New Delhi: Prentice Hall, 1965.

4

Social Change

Rise of Popular Culture

The extent to which western lifestyle has penetrated into the cultural stream of India or the degree to which our youth have undergone normative transformation, can be analyzed only in the perspective of overall cultural and social changes that have taken place in our society during the past 50 years. The processes of empowerment of women can also be located within these societal and cultural aspects of change. Yet, we could not objectively evaluate these processes without grounding our analysis on the foundation of the ideology of social change in India since independence. No doubt, some intellectuals have expressed doubt as to whether India could evolve a coherent ideology of change, it is doubtful if any society can undergo changes and remain integrated if it is devoid of a meaningful ideology. The issues of ideology assume significance when we attempt to understand the manner in which the western lifestyle has become pervasive in our society and particularly among the youth, or if at all the road to empowerment of women in India has now been paved smooth and strong.

The two concepts which have often been counterposed in the debate on the ideology of social change are westernization and modernization. This debate runs through the entire gamut of the various movements for cultural renaissance of India since the beginning of the British rule. It permeates the values of our national leadership during the freedom movement. The contributions of Gandhi and Nehru reflect this process accepting that these two represented two different ideologies of modernization. One may yet notice a fair measure of ambivalence towards westernization in the thinking of both, as both felt strongly that modernization of our society does not imply our mindless imitation of the West or total rejection of our tradition. Of course, that part of tradition which has become obsolete or which militates against the spirit of humanism needs to be dropped, and all that is noble in it must be integrated in the modernization paradigm of society. Their notion of tradition was not merely textual. It encompassed, on the contrary, the entire range of the living tradition of the Indian people (peasants, tribals, minorities, etc.) as nurtured through centuries and reflected in its artforms, aesthetic traditions, folk culture, tribal culture and other artistic expressions, etc. Nehru was particularly sensitive to protecting and preserving these traditions and in adaptively integrating them in our institutions and values as we proceed towards cultural and social modernization. Gandhi's emphasis on decentralization and communitarian self-rule had also implicitly recognized the pre-eminence of the local indigenous traditions.

Is modernization without westernization possible? In what sense are the two terms conceptually distinct? Could one outline concrete indicators of the two processes to measure differences? Social scientists in India have debated these points for several decades. Sometimes, a distinction between modernization and westernization is made on the basis that westernization is an empirically observable phenomenon in the behaviour and lifestyle of the people whereas modernization is an ideological concept. However, it is not easy to spell out the characteristics of modernization as an ideology. Modernization is a form of rationalization through which introduction of a whole range of social and cultural changes in societies is legitimated. Social scientists have worked out empirical indicators of modernization. These too, however, remain in the realm of rationalization since even to this date no universally accepted sets of modernization indicators exist. Now, even the notion of modernity is being challenged and seems to be on the retreat.

CONTINUITY, IDENTITY AND CHANGE

A significant quality of social change which relates to structures and processes in societies is that of continuity and resilience of the traditional institutions and values. The processes of westernization and modernization have both encountered this phenomenon in all societies. Why is it that despite the overwhelming changes in structures and institutions societies do preserve many elements of their cultural styles, modes of living and the normative and cognitive patterns of thinking? Why is it that despite radical legislative measures to bring about change, the norms of social hierarchy, degree of empowerment of women and the extent of religious and cultural tolerance remain confounded? Culture changes only slowly and adaptively. Social anthropologists have variously explained it as being a result of the fact that a culture is always integratively constituted. Each culture has a basic 'theme' or 'pattern' or 'symbolic code' which constitutes its core, and all changes in it are mediated by it. The continuity of culture is also associated with the formation of 'identities' in the 'basic personality structures' of the members of society which are influenced by techno-economy, socialization process in the family, particularly the role of the mother in socialization of child, and the nature of social differentiation in societies. These factors define the limits of ideology in bringing about social change---sponsored as well as self-generated.

As to the extent to which our youth in particular and people in general are tending to accept the western lifestyle or the 'norms of modernity', these aspects of cultural change become relevant. We have to be careful in distinguishing between the 'appearance' of change or its surface manifestation and the 'deeper' levels of change through accommodation or integration of cultural traits with the pre-existing cultural patterns. We have also to correlate it with the structure of identities of persons concerned who are members of different cultural and sub-cultural groups. An important substantive problem here relates to the processes of differentiation within the cultural patterns. It largely corresponds with the evolution in its modes of production and the information technology in societies.

In the pre-industrial India, dominated by the feudal mode of production, there was differentiation in the cultural styles and forms between the folk and the elite cultures. The peasants and workers belonged to the folk cultural tradition which was primarily oral, community-(caste-tribe) based and was carried through from generation to generation adapting itself and always accommodating new currents with spontaneity and creativity. Folk culture was, of course, in constant interaction with the elite cultural tradition which was textual, formal and systematic. There existed between the two a process of reciprocity in the adoption and adaptation of styles, themes and forms. For this reason, folk cultural tradition has also been described as 'part-culture'. This traditional mode of culture was entrenched into the organic bases of the traditional social structures such as the caste, tribe and community. The peasant and feudal economy, being relatively stable in respect of technology and social institutions, the folk-elite culture continued not only to integrate new cultures and styles of life within the established traditions but also protected it from erosion so long as the traditional economic and social structures persisted. It had enormous resilience to assimilate and integrate the alien cultural forms and styles.

As the nature of the traditional agrarian-feudal economy undergoes capitalist, market-oriented transformation and as the traditional social structures which legitimized access to culture-forms, styles and roles in accordance with one's position in the class (peasant-worker) and caste hierarchy undergo changes due to politicization and democratization of the traditional communitarian structures of the villages and the cities, a new form of cultural differentiation takes place. This has been variously described as 'popular culture' or 'mass culture'. Its emergence coincides with the revolutionary changes in the technology-base of communication and leads to the expansion of mass media on one hand and growth in transport and travel facilities on the other. These technological innovations intensify the volume and velocity of the communication of people, cultures and styles of life. The popular culture, unlike the folk-elite culture-form, is not based on the communitarian social structures institutionalized by custom and tradition. It is not even territorially bounded. Its form, style and representation are not governed by pre-set traditional rules or customary definitions but by free-floating market forces.

Popular culture derives its legitimation not from the conformity with the *shastric* or formal norms or standards but from the impulse to manipulate or engineer people's motivations to augment the market forces for profit. Its aesthetics is essentially eclectic. It is, however, technologically unmatched in the power of self-augmentation, expansion and domination as it rides on the wings of the print and electronic media. For patronage, it does not have to depend upon solidary communities or other institutionalized social groups as all traditional cultural institutions did. It creates patrons on its own through a new social phenomenon called 'audience' which is neither a community nor a group. Audience is a faceless agglomeration of individuals who for a certain moment of time share commonality of viewership or audio-experience of mass media through their exposure to the messages or symbols having 'cultural significance' in a broad sense. Forms of advertisement, calendar art, popular cinema, telefilms, documentaries, etc., constitute its one aspect and the cultural programmes beamed through radio and television represent its other manifestation.

The growth of popular culture coincides with deeper social transformation in society. The indicators of this change are: disenchantment with the traditional rural life, massive migration to the cities, growing charm for consumerism, tremendous expansion of the psychic and social mobility of people with corresponding weakening of the bonds within family, kin group and the local communities. Popular culture also coincides with the rise of individualism and individual's search for perpetual renewal of experiences. With the expansion of market and the globalization of media, the clout of popular culture eventually has a disruptive influence both upon the folk and elite forms of traditional culture. Culture is then increasingly converted into commodity. Not its content but its packaging and marketability matters the most. It tends to become more alluring as it offers to the traditional artists enormous profit and publicity for their consent to be incorporated after having destroyed their traditional social base. Popular culture alienates not only the artist from his art forms but also art from its organic link with the community. It abstracts culture for the media of work, fractures its aesthetic expressiveness, and distorts the dialectic of its sacred-secular worldview. Obviously, these changes coincide with changes in the social structure ushered in by the march of industrialization, urbanization and the expansion of media and information in society. The two institutions which get deeply impacted by these changes are family and community. The erosion of their influence upon the youth creates a situation in which discrepant choices of cultural norms and artifacts are rendered possible. The expanding role of the popular or mass culture further reinforces this process.

Serious questions in this context arise on the issues of cultural identity, continuity and change. The structural base of the traditional folk-elite pattern of culture, which depended upon traditional technology, mode of production and social hierarchy, is turned upside down as it is impacted by the techno-economic forces and institutions of a post-industrial information society in the making. The capacity of traditional societies to assimilate new elements of popular culture in their own pattern through adaptive capability is now rendered most difficult.

TRADITIONAL AND WESTERN STYLES OF LIFE

These changes constitute the necessary backdrop for the analysis of the impact of the western style of life upon our people, particularly the youth. However, the image of the traditional Indian culture in contradiction to that of the West also needs to be corrected. A view popular both in India and the West is that the Indian culture is rooted in asceticism and other-worldiness. The western culture, in contrast, is held to be entirely materialistic and this-worldly. Most Indians are supposed to be non-materialistic or engrossed in spiritual pursuits of one kind or the other. The institution of caste and the traditional social systems such as family and community are thought to be products entirely of moral legitimations totally unrelated to their principles of power and control over the material resources. Despite wider recognition of cultural pluralism in India or even the presence of a materialist tradition in the Hindu philosophy, the image of India being an ascetic and other-worldly nation has stuck as a stereotype in our analysis of westernization. Our assessment of the challenges that westernization or the expansion of the western style of life poses to India is often unrealistic due to this stereotyped categorization.

Partly this evaluation is a result of depending heavily on the textual sources of the Indian tradition for an insight into its culture and style of life. Now, the regional studies and surveys of the villages and cities give us reliable insights into our people's culture traits, customs and lifestyle. Their findings contradict the stereotype about Indians' asceticism. A survey of the 4,634 communities, representing all the communities living in India, completed by the Anthropological Survey of India, has concluded:

> "Alcoholic beverages are consumed by men in the communities studied as follows: occasionally in 2,469 and regularly in 1,106. Women occasionally consume alcohol in 1,037 communities. Smoking is very common. Chewing of tobacco and the use of snuff are also widespread. Chewing of betel is used by people in large number of communities. We are, therefore, largely a drinking, smoking and meat-eating people."

Various rounds of the National Sample Survey data on consumption offer us enough corroborative evidences to the effect that major changes in people's style of life (both in the villages and the cities) and habits of consumption are taking place. Consumption of eggs and poultry, considered a taboo among both the upper and middle (peasant) caste Hindus a few decades ago, has become widespread throughout the country. Non-vegetarianism among the traditionally vegetarian peasant castes and the Brahmins has been increasing. Along with changes in the food habits significant changes in the patterns of dresses, uses of cosmetics and new materials in utensils and cooking appliances, etc., have taken place. The new modes of communication, means of leisure and recreation are fast replacing the older ones. Most aspects of these changes incorporate elements of the western style of life and culture. But these occur piecemeal and not as a system. The traits of the western culture are making their way into our cultural life but the extent to which they have a potential to alter the systemic cultural world-view remains a matter of surmise.

WESTERN STYLE OF LIFE: THE PAST AND THE PRESENT

Historically, from the early nineteenth century onwards, the Indian people, particularly the elite, came under the western political domination. This brought into its terrain the process of cultural encounter. The national movement that culminated over several other movements towards cultural renaissance, evolved a cultural strategy to resolve the dilemma of westernization and this strategy was to modernize India without total westernization---this goal became the cultural policy of free India. The state directly sponsored several cultural institutions, practices and policies to articulate and strengthen the best elements of the Indian cultural tradition. Nevertheless, the contact with the West did usher in many western cultural traits and practices over a period of time. Due to peculiar nature of the Indian social structure based on caste and sub-castes, its vast regional cultural diversities and cultural differences between the rural and the urban centres, the initial process of westernization of the lifestyle was confined to a small section of urban elite. It existed as a sub-culture. This remained so up to the period of independence. This sub-culture extended to include lifestyle as well as western literature, philosophy and art. Its impact could be seen in the nineteenth century literary contributions in India not only in Bengali but also in Marathi, Tamil and Telugu languages. The vigorous debates on the rationalist-positivist philosophy of the West informed many literary and social science writings of this time. The exposure was thus not only to the western lifestyle but also to its philosophy and worldview.

The sub-culture of the western lifestyle slowly began to expand in India due to new emerging processes of social change. These were: expansion of new technologies of transport and communication such as the railways, roadways and post and telegraph services; establishment of several western institutions such as a rational administration, judiciary, legal system, educational institutions, and the like. The beginning of census operations and land settlements, together with many research and survey operations, generated information and exposed Indians to new methods of administration and new outlooks. The pace of westernization, however, began to increase due to these exposures which influenced the modes of trade, employment and education.

The national movement for independence, based on the Gandhian strategy of *swadeshi* (to use only the indigenously made consumption goods), did retard for a time the rapid expansion of the western style of consumption and living. But its impact began to weaken fast soon after independence. Several sociological studies about the changes in values and styles of living conducted during the 1950s and 1960s illustrate significant changes taking place in the lifestyle mainly due to the contact with the urban centres, increased incidence of travel and the technological modernization of the production of commodities of mass consumption. Its impact upon the traditional customs and rituals have also been very substantial. In his study of a Mysore village, M.N. Srinivas noted:

> "The westernization of the Brahmins of Mysore brought about a number of changes in their life. There was change in their appearance and dress. The tuft gave way to cropped hair and the traditional dress gave place, at least partially, to western type dress and shoes. The change in dress marked a gradual weakening of ideas regarding ritual purity. For instance, formerly eating was a ritual act, and a Brahmin had to wear ritually pure robes while eating or serving meals. This meant wearing either a freshly washed cotton *dhoti* or a silk *dhoti*, and a pure upper cloth. Wearing a shirt was taboo. But as western clothes became more popular, Brahmins sat at their dinner with their shirts on. And today, dining at a table is becoming common among the rich."

Similar changes in aspects of lifestyle of people have been reported for several other regions in the country.

During the past 50 years, the impact of the western lifestyle upon people in India has continued to increase and expand. How deep is this influence can be a matter of debate. It is also questionable as to how far it restructures the cultural identity of the Indians in a western mould. One is also not sure as to how the western style of life, which has certainly expanded in sc and coverage, succeeds in displacing the core values of the traditional Indian culture.

But, in these five decades, many significant changes have taken place in social structure of the Indian society. The application of modern technology in agriculture has contributed to the rise of a rich middle class peasantry. The reservation policy in education and governmental jobs in favour of the scheduled castes and scheduled tribes, has triggered social mobility among them and a vocal leadership has emerged. Dalit movement, a product of the new agenda of cultural renaissance among the traditionally exploited lower castes, also challenged many tenets of traditional Brahmanical culture. It openly denigrated the principles of Hindu *dharmashastras* (religious scriptures). Forty years of sustained planning by the state has created a substantial urban middle class in the service sector, the professions and in business and entrepreneurial activities. The size of the middle classes in India is now estimated to range from 200 to 300 million. Also, the population which has been constantly rising may soon reach a billion mark. With high rate of growth in population, the proportion of youth has now a domineering presence. The enfranchisement of youth, between 18 and 21 year of age, adds a political dimension to this process of change. The scale of urbanization has also increased. The number of cities with a population of a million or more has seen phenomenal rise; the growth in the metropolitan cities is recorded as being the highest. The bigger the population of a city, the higher is its rate of immigration, and this indicates uneven levels of available job opportunities and developmental activities in our cities. Overarching these social structural changes, the process of change is further accelerated due to the pervasive influence of information media such as radio, television, newspapers and magazines. Almost every household has a radio set now. Possession of television and subscription to newspapers and magazines is as yet limited but considering the size of the middle classes and the multiplier effect of circulation, their influence is substantial.

These changes reveal how during the span of the past 50 years the process of social and psychic mobility of our people has undergone changes which expands the sub-cultural base of westernization. The youth constitute a very dominant category of this population. This is first, because of the nature of demographic transition in India with high population growth rate and secondly, because youth constitute, by their very nature, a sociologically vulnerable category. Their vulnerability has also been compounded because of the structural and cultural tensions to which they are now exposed due to the changes in the family and the community organizations and their functions. Due to over-politicization of caste and religion, the village communities have turned into factious political communities. The new *Panchayati Raj* (village council administration) is entirely cast on the political mould. The institution of family now increasingly faces pressures of fission due to economic, cultural and social reorientation of its functions and obligations. It has brought about major changes in the values, aspirations and cultural preferences of the youth and women in India.

NORMS OF MODERN YOUTH AND THE WESTERN LIFESTYLE

Obviously, the norms and lifestyle of youth in contemporary India bear a deep impact of the changes in society, its social structure and values. The role played by the political institutions and ideologies and the changes in the agrarian and industrial economy have largely contributed to the emergence of a new scale of values by which the youth today perceive their aspiration for the future. No doubt, the elements of the western culture and lifestyle occupy much space in the cultural life of the youth today. How far these preferences for the western lifestyle constitute an integral part of their cultural worldview is as yet questionable. The scope of the spread of the western forms of lifestyle observable by youth's acceptance of the western foods and beverages, dress, cosmetics and ornamentations, music, dance and artifacts is now very substantial. The western style of living, such as internal furnishing and stylizing of household, reading of western journals, magazines and literature, has grown very fast. The western values and practices have also been adopted by youth in interpersonal relationship. The practice of dating and acceptance of new values regarding sexual relationship and marriage are now more common. In metropolitan cities one may also come across professional young couples 'living together' without entering into matrimony. This trend may further increase in the future as the burden of metropolitan living and pressure of work becomes more and more demanding in the context of high rise in consumerism and individualism.

Of the total Indian population only about one-third lives in the cities. The rate of urbanization is uneven among different states in India. States like Bihar, Orissa and Assam have only about 15 per cent urban population. In Punjab, Maharashtra, Gujarat, Tamil Nadu and Karnataka, 30 per cent people live in the cities. Obviously, India is still a rural society, and the nature of its urban spread is regionalized. The intensity of the urban cultural influences is concentrated in the major metropolitan cities, like Delhi, Calcutta, Chennai, Mumbai and Bangalore. The legitimacy or the culture of the western lifestyle for the youth, even in these metropolises, is governed by the historicity of the regional cultural traditions. No doubt, a sub-culture of youth has grown in these cities which celebrates western style of life. It covers their preference for western food, dress, recreation, art, music, sexual relations and the style of living. Yet, this sub-culture is confined mainly to the youth coming from the educated urban middle classes. Its extent is limited but its significance lies not in its magnitude but its appeal to youth all over in the villages and to the classes lower in the scheme of social stratification.

The new forces of social change, politicization and media exposure have changed youths' values and social psychology throughout the country, from the village to the town and to the metropolis. Youth are disenchanted from the present state of things around them and seek opportunities outside. The rural youth wish to migrate to the cities, whereas the urban youth, particularly those from the middle classes and the upper castes (for whom reservation policy has now made access to government jobs limited in scope), wish either to seek employment in lucrative private sector jobs or migrate outside the country. The globalization of economy, and the decentralization of production of goods and services by the multinational corporations, have totally altered for these youth the project of their future and the perception of their 'life-world'. The 'success theme' has become universal, and the successful performers are the youth who are perceived to have imbibed the western lifestyle to the maximum extent.

Most of these youths are products of professional institutions and come from the urban middle class family background. The youths belonging to the rural middle class peasantry (mostly belonging to the backward classes), who have newly acquired political influence and wealth due to the Green Revolution in agriculture, are also disenchanted. This is because they do not see chances of a better life in farming or in rural life. Due to poor technology and rising per unit cost of production, agriculture as an occupation has become hazardous and non-profitable. The pressure of population in the family over a few generations has led to fragmentation of landholdings. Bigger units of farms have become smaller and unviable leading to farmers' loss of social and economic status. The absence of opportunities of employment outside agriculture makes the situation worse. Also, the quality of life in the villages remains abysmally poor. Hence, the rural youth search for opportunities outside and are intensely involved in the politics of backward class movement or Dalit movement in all parts of the country.

Another important tension in the values of the youth is reflected in the change in their attitude towards authority—be it in the family or the public institutions or the state. In rural areas, older generation parents lost much of their authority due to 'technology-information' and 'management-market' orientation in agriculture following the Green Revolution. Continual learning and experimentation and not knowledge acquired by age was now required. From the decade of 1970s onwards, the decision-making power shifted from their old patriarch to his younger sons who may be a semi-literate or a school-college dropout. We also see composition of the *panchayat* leadership in various parts of the country shifting in favour of the youth or youthful adults around this period. In the urban families too major changes in the structure of authority take place due to the pressure on younger people to show initiative early in their student career (from higher secondary to bachelor's course) for preparing themselves for better jobs. In the changed context, not the degree as much as the training, exposure, initiative and experience get the premium. Many values of the parents' generation in regard to education and employment are now put in jeopardy, especially in the middle class urban families. It erodes the traditional mystique of the parental authority and guidance defining youths' aspirations, their lifestyle and future planning.

These structural changes have imparted much freedom to the youth to define their life aspirations and lifestyle. Moreover, the family institutions that provide normative stability to the youth, are under great structural and functional stress, both in the cities and the villages. It may not, however, suggest that the traditional family values of loyalty towards parents, parental support to children or the traditional values in regard to marriage and customary rites or rituals have withered away. They continue to persist in most parts of the country and in large majority of families. However, the spread of youth's lure for western lifestyle is incrementally gaining ground. The nature and extent of this westernization of lifestyle varies in terms of rural-urban and class-caste composition.

WESTERN LIFESTYLE OF YOUTH AND ITS FUTURE

We have noted earlier how in order that cultural changes become stable or get institutionalized in a society they must get integrated with society's 'pattern' of culture, or its systemic core values. For an individual new values or cultural styles constitute a part of his/her cultural identity and worldview. From this premise the future of the westernization process of the Indian youth can be evaluated. Does the impact of the western lifestyle on the youth constitute a transformation of their worldview and identity? Do the cultural elements selectively taken from the West enjoy cultural autonomy? Do they constitute a separate culture pattern? Do these western traits subsist in the youth's life as a congery of culture traits or constitute a meaningfully coherent system?

We need to answer these questions before we could forecast about the future of westernization of the lifestyle of youth. In an analysis of these issues in the larger context of Indian society during the 1970s, we had found that the westernization and modernization processes in India did not replace tradition. Through selective incorporation of the western values, ideas, technologies and institutions, etc., the tradition itself underwent transformation. This factual situation has its basis in logic. The cultural patterns in each society are historically conditioned and comprise values at two levels: instrumental and categorical. Cultural changes begin with changes first, in instrument values, such as economy, technology, patterns of consumption and living styles, etc.

But changes in the core values of the culture which belong to the independent or categorical structure of values of a society, and constitute cultural identities of its people, do not undergo total transformation. It changes slowly as it adapts itself to new values. Identities are deeply rooted in individual psyche and constitute a symbolic configuration of passions and meanings culturally mediated by socialization in the childhood. "A sense of identity means a sense of being at one with oneself as one grows and develops; and it means, at the same time, a sense of affinity with a community's sense of being at one with its future as well as its history---or mythology," says Erik H. Erikson. He further adds that "twenty years is about the span of development needed for the individual to acquire a sense of identity, firm and informed enough to act: which requires enough experience to acknowledge the power of facts and facts of power, enough practical idealism to attach infantile ideals to live persons and issues, and enough rebellious commitment to the future to leave behind some of the internalized debt of infantile guilt." At this stage, both 'affiliative bonds' and 'antagonistic exclusions' are resorted to by youth acting through the given cultural configuration.

The youth of twenty years and above in our country grew up as children during the decade of 1970s, a most turbulent and yet politically cathartic period of our history. It was a period of political and social turmoils when the Emergency was lifted and democracy restored. It was during this time when the Mandal Commission on the Backward Classes recommended 27 per cent reservation in the Central Government services for the backward classes, enhancing the anxieties and cleavages of the upper caste/class youth. This strengthened the disenchantment from the existing system of a large majority of the upper caste, middle class youth in the country. Even otherwise, the youth in general felt betrayed by many events during the past decade. The decline in the political values of men in public life, the preference for patronage to merit in public services and enterprises, the increasing rate of criminalization of politics and corruption in daily life, etc., bred an anxiety syndrome among the youth which only reinforced their ethical calculus in favour of being more 'expedient' than 'principled'. Their fragile ethical code only got reinforced by the emerging western lifestyles on one hand, and on the other, all too strong affiliative bonds with one's caste, ethnicity and religion. Consequently, youth's identity today tends to be internally fragmented by contradictions.

This explains why their preference for western lifestyle in one instance and their pull towards traditional rituals and religious beliefs at other occasion have for them pertinence even though apparently contradictory. Youth are continually making pragmatic reconciliation between the two which may explain the self-encapsulating nature of their westernization.

The youth may not have renounced their search for adaptive cultural adjustment between tradition and westernization. There is enough sociological evidence to support this conclusion. As the cultural space of westernization is expanding, we also witness counter-westernization movements in all parts of the country. There is tremendous growth in youth's commitment to cosmopolitan values, and yet the hold of caste, ethnicity and religion remains intact. Moreover, the power of western culture and its worldview based on rationality, humanism and freedom—all aspects of the renaissance ideology—seem to have developed cracks even in the West. The wave of post-modernism is symptomatic of the anxieties in the West on account of disintegration of family and community life. Today, unlike in the eighteenth and nineteenth century, an Indian's encounter with the West is qualitatively different. As a cultural alternative or a coherent worldview, the post-industrial and post-modern West is not certain of itself and is groping for a new way out of its own social and cultural dilemmas. This should further confound the impact of the western influences on our youth. The impact of the western style of life on our youth may, therefore, continue to remain adaptive rather than substitutive in nature, between tradition and modernity.

SOCIAL CHANGE AND EMPOWERMENT OF WOMEN

The notion of empowerment has had a wider connotation as it emerged as a social movement ideology of the blacks and marginalized groups focusing on access to resources, freedom of choice-making in occupation, education, health, housing and social relationships. It also implied enabling the marginalized and discriminated sections of society to gain self-generating power to be equal partners in the process of development, removal of vulnerability to exploitation and prevention of violence and injustices perpetrated upon them. It also implied cultivating self-consciousness about the iniquitous and exploitative control of state and its organs of power in the areas of health, ecology, technology, strategies of economic-industrial development and mobilization of the affected people. Ecological and environmental movements particularly belong to this category. During the past 50 years, a large number of such movements have started and the study of these movements has generated substantial amount of information and insight into social science.

Empowerment of women conceptually forms a distinct category by itself. It implies processes by which women's power of self-organization is promoted and reinforced, they develop the capacity for self-reliance outcrossing the relationship of subordination on account of gender, social and economic status and the role in the family and society. It encompasses their ability to make choices, control resources and enjoy participatory relationship within, family and community. To achieve these objectives empowerment of women also implies their ability to consolidate social movements to remove obstacles in their path, be it from state and administration, family and kinship, workplace and its organization, institutions of production of culture and knowledge or arenas of politics and power.

The movement for the empowerment of women and its ideology has undergone significant differentiation in India since the time of the national movement, which was the first systematic effort in our country to bring women in the foreground of the national level participation in the activities of social, economic and political regeneration of society. This movement threw up a leadership among the women and also deeply influenced their role perception over the following decades. Commensurate with these objectives many legislative changes were introduced. The past 50 years reflect some basic changes in the status and role of women in our society. Now, this process is further accelerated since some are becoming increasingly self-conscious of their discrimination in several areas of family and public life. They are also today in a position to mobilize themselves on issues which affect them vitally, and constitute a significant segment in the electoral politics of our nation. The establishment of a national commission to monitor the status of women, reservation of 33 per cent of seats in the village *panchayats* (councils) through a constitutional amendment and the measures being contemplated to reserve 33 per cent of seats for women in the parliament and the state assemblies testify to the increasing recognition of the role of women in the power structure of our society.

The movement for the empowerment of women that started during the national movement, was in ideological terms co-optational and generalized. The new movements for empowerment of women are increasingly particularistic and focus entirely on the condition of women as a separate entity. Studies of empowerment of women all over the world have revealed that the effort towards their empowerment succeeds only when attention is invited by women through their self-managed and self-sustained organizational and movement-oriented activities and not when the agenda for empowerment is made a part of the general development plan of society. Women's movement for self-empowerment today differs materially in this regard from the then strategy evolved by leadership of the national movement. Nevertheless, this movement did also contribute to several women-specific schemes and projects for their empowerment. Several activist groups and the voluntary associations started during the national movement are even now doing most effective work towards the empowerment of women in our society.

A worrisome aspect of the social movements and the development policies for the empowerment of women in our society refers to glaring difference between the ideological or the institutional response to the problem and the concrete achievements or results. This difference is also reflected in the census surveys. It is revealed that during the past decades sex ratio in the country has been continuously worsening. The illiteracy among women is endemic being 36 per cent compared to 64.3 per cent among men. With the exception of Kerala where the female literacy is 86.9 per cent, in states like Bihar, Rajasthan, Uttar Pradesh and Madhya Pradesh less than 30 per cent women are literate, whereas almost three-fourth of our population is concentrated in this region. The report prepared by the United Nations Development Programme (UNDP) places India at 103 out of 174 in the rank of "gender-related development index". On "gender empowerment measure", India ranks 93 while China ranks 29, Indonesia 61 and even its neighbours Nepal and Bhutan score better. Literacy is the most effective instrument of self-empowerment. If a society denies this right to most of its women, all its other claims towards taking steps for the empowerment of women are easily nullified.

This discrepancy in the ideology and practice of the empowerment policy of women in our country constitutes the foundation of India's continued social, economic and cultural backwardness. It tells adversely upon effective implementation of the policies on population, health, child care and ecology development. These, as we know, are the building blocks of social and economic growth and modernization of society. Deprivation of women reinforces the social and cultural prejudices on gender issues in society. The female child is often denied the basic right to survival and most female children are given a second class status in terms of human rights. The empowerment of women in a society is most effective index of measuring modernization and development. In India, we have to traverse a long distance to achieve this goal.

To sum up, since independence major social and cultural changes have taken place in India. Socially, the country h achieved a significant measure of status mobility among the traditionally underprivileged classes. The middle classes and castes have emerged as a powerful political force. People's level of aspiration and their motivation to enhance their social, economic and cultural status has risen so high that it often causes mismatch between the aspiration and the opportunity to achieve it. This generates continual tension, unrest and even violence and crime. It also fuels militant movements. The structural change, particularly social and economic growth, is not evenly distributed among regions. It creates a potential for increased regional conflicts in the future. Also, the change has given rise to the emergence of a very significant section of the westernized elite and youth who often, being unable to find stable cultural mooring and succourance in the family or community, perceive their adult generation to be a fractured role model. This double instability breeds a tendency among youth either to culturally drift or turn resentful of what they perceive around them. One manifestation of this is found in their fetishism of some aspects of the western culture. Otherwise, westernization is proceeding selectively in India through an adaptive process. Its scope today seems much extended only because the middle class base in our society has grown larger as never before.

5

Myth, History and Reason

Culture and Nation-Building in India

Culture has its roots in the phenomenology of species. It is deeply anchored in the existential aspects of human reality, and one cannot go far in understanding culture or the relationship that culture has with the society without locating in the existential milieu.

There are, however, certain elements in the human reality which go beyond the existential; those are cognitive, symbolic and mental. These elements enjoy a certain degree of autonomy over the existential. In the process of being human within the context of the existential the dynamics of culture and symbolic life is involved. To enrich this process interactions between the symbolic and the material aspects of life are necessary. Its quality determines the degree of evolution of culture. I see a very definite relationship between different modes of production and the cultural styles and patterns. The transition from the tribal to peasant-folk and to the contemporary techno-industrial culture reflects this process. Now we are entering into the phase of information society and 'popular culture'.

When we look at this dynamics we also notice that culture cannot be contained and it militates against any paradigm of reductionism. All of culture is not merely organic. There exists in human reality a potential which goes beyond the organic, people have given it different names at different times. The dynamics of culture manifests itself at three levels where different principles are involved. The first principle is that of mythology, myth making is a very unique attribute of the humankind. Then, there is history and the principle of historiography through which events of social significance are given meanings. Thirdly, there is the principle of reason or logic which influences the instrumental aspects of life. Myth, history and logic or reason together subsume and manifest the human potential.

They may be subjectively located but are essentially reflected through a collective pattern and social power. Myth is a powerful social reality. It exudes power over human beings and is independent of them as it governs the behaviour and thinking of a large aggregate of human kind. It is a collective creation of humankind and yet it confronts humanity as an independent reality. Myth is an important phenomenon that influences the social institutions, and there always exists a critical relationship between history and mythology. A lot of history in course of time is transformed into mythology. Ideologies flourish in the ambiguous spaces between mythology and history. Finally, there is the principle of logic, science and reason. These rely upon the validity and verifiability of instrumental values in the functioning of social processes.

One cannot understand the relationship between culture and nation-building without analyzing the relative impact of these three principles, as they interact and are reflected upon the structure and function of the entities which constitute the nation. It is a critical yet a defining aspect of the processes we call 'nation-building'. A very important aspect of the relationship among myth, history and reason is that in theoretical terms it goes beyond the metaphors of tradition and modernity. Sometimes we think that the modern society which lives entirely in the space of reason, is disenchanted from the principle of myth. The principles of history, science and logic are of course central to the concept of modernization as reflected in the nation-building process. But what about myth? A paradox of human condition today is that myth never dies. The dynamic and intricate relationships among myth, history and reason continue to prevail. It only changes its form. So what is described as the movement from tradition to modernity in nation-building is not a replacement of this triadic pattern of relationships among myth, history and reason but a qualitative reconfiguration of the internal structure of their relationships.

We may ask: do modern societies have myths? In fact, modern societies thrive on mythology. One example of modern myth is advertisements which we see everyday on our television. All of us know that these are different in real-life situations and are deliberately contrived for consumer attraction. The major motivation is for gaining the market. Facts are presented often in a distorted form. Thus, the modern media creates mythology of its own. Very often even the press constructs mythological realities. The facts and events (history) are presented-represented selectively, and people begin to believe in them as a matter of intrinsic faith very much as they believe in myths. Even the world of science at the cultural level is not free from mythology because most people do not understand even the first principles of science and yet they are overwhelmed by its operational manifestations (technology) and harbour faith in them; science thus creates its mythology as it were. So is the case with history. There is the myth of purity of the Aryan race. It became the basis of anthropological and historical researches in Germany during the Nazi regime.

As we move from this dimension of relationships between the existential level of culture or its symbolic expressions to the roles of history, myth and reason in the process of formation of the modern state, the dilemmas do not come to an end. We see that the reality of the modern society and the notion of modernity are so complex that depending wholly on its notion or paradigm we are not going to solve our problems. Modernity only poses new challenges probably more formidable which we will have to overcome. The nation-building process is one such challenge. Moreover, the contours of modernity are now being redefined. We are moving from reality to virtual reality, which is full of hazards. On the one hand, it reinforces scientific imagination and on the other, it encourages obscenity and degeneration. We can choose today in the cyberspace anything of our volition which more often than not militates against reason. Thus, the dilemma of modern society is rendered more complex.

THE NATION-STATE

Nation as a concept is very complex. It may not be easy to define a nation. There is always the danger of reification. We know about the controversy in philosophy on the definition of mind. What is mind? The attributional answers to the question could not have resolved the difficulty, so an operational definition was offered that mind is 'minding'. Mind is a process of intellection. Our approach to the definition of nation is to look at is operationally. Nation is a process. We call this process nation-building, and then of about finding out how this process is taking place, what are its elements, what are its strengths and weaknesses. In the process of nation-building we find two different ways in which triadic factors, viz., myth, history and reason have worked. Both ways are important and have a base.

One way is towards the evolution and the growth of reason, i.e., growth is science, productive capacity, evolution from hunting and food gathering, mode of production to agricultural mode of production and then on to the industrial and finally to the post-industrial mode of production. In India, we are moving from agricultural to the industrial mode of production, and there is some beginning of the early stages of the post-industrial, information-oriented society. There is growth in the professional and managerial areas that need to be studied. However these changes which relate to the economic structure of the society or its related utilitarian domains of structures and values can be easily assigned to the rational space of nation-building. The scope for mythification is limited at this level, although it cannot be totally denied. Much of the dilemma of the modern nation-building process not only in India but in most other societies is that continual difficulties arise as to how to integrate mythical with the historical and the rational. The mythical and historical consciousness pull societies towards segmentation of social boundaries and are essentially self-limiting in character. It generates consciousness which is primarily anchored in the notion of identity----temporarily or historically. These keep on creating enclaves of cultural symbols and styles. This process, ironically, does not weaken with the march of reason and economic growth. The economic growth, particularly when its fruits are uneven, gives rise to interest groups which delight in the celebration within the mythical space. It is a dilemma which has not come to an end even in the modern societies where the level of prosperity is high. The tensions arising out of the mythic mode of thinking are located in primordiality, in religion, in ethnicity, in tribalism and in neo-tribalism seen as emergent today. So, the problem of nation-building in India is located, on the one hand, in the evolutionary integrative processes of economy and profession through which the rationalization of the productive forces takes place, and on the other, it can also be observed at the level of the emergent forces of segmentation.

The interest group organizations also play a significant role in the modern myth-making The solution lies in competing organizations. If an advertisement is wrong or is misleading, then it is the consumer movement that takes care of it. Here, the consumer group movement works as an interest group which acts as corrective to the mythology of modern communication media. If the communication media becomes mythological we have an organization which takes care of it. Similarly, in the traditional societies when mythologies acted against the existential interests of the people, new dissenters as groups or individual would arise. Usually, the modality was the emergence of either a new sect led by a prophet or reform movements within the interest groups which propagated a discrepant mythology. Thus, the tussle between organizations located in their existential interests and those that were anchored in the symbolic space in life have existed and are bound to go on. The nation-building process in India or elsewhere would have to come to terms with these realities and from this perspective the problem of nation-building relates to the process of institution-building which is responsive to accommodate interest groups at levels both existential and symbolic.

In a relatively less developed nation such as India when the productive forces are not garnered properly and the distribution of resources is not done effectively, the mobilizing interest groups emerging from different segments of the society create serious dislocation. A nation cannot sustain itself and remain intact without augmenting strong productive forces followed by effective distributive mechanisms. Production and distribution at an accelerated pace are very important elements in the nation-building process. Not only it helps integrate mythology with reason but also creates functional links among interest groups. Therefore, we may be sure that any paradigm of nation-building which is based entirely on mythical uses of culture is not going to be sufficient for successful nation-building. A corollary of this observation is that religion cannot be the basis of nation-building in India. Similarly, mere articulation of primordiality, such as caste and ethnicity, cannot be the basis of nation-building process. Yet, the existence of primordial identities should not only be treated as normal but protected. The respect for local culture, local customs and history, etc., constitute the dynamic elements which give support to the process of nation-building.

Between culture and nation-building there is a link issue of the quality of life. To promote quality of life the growth of huge industries or a movement from the industrial to the post-industrial phase of growth which encourages consumerism and environmental decay is not sufficient. To counter-balance the social and emotional dislocations of the industrial society it is necessary to promote privacy in life, memories, mythologies, fantasies and religious beliefs of people at the level of local cultures. Nevertheless, being segmentary in nature, these factors alone cannot, in a country like India which has so many distinct levels of identities, form the major principles of nation-building. This is important and, therefore, the institutions of democracy and civil society will have to be strengthened. Local and smaller cultural space may still be required. This is evident from the fact that developed societies in Europe and North America today lament for the loss of primary groups, family, community, etc. We in India have to be forewarned. There is a possibility of these institutions becoming weaker also in our country and the process has already started. It is not necessary, therefore, that the mythic or historical and primordial identities be neglected. In fact, the growth of the primordial segment should reinforce and add strength to the structures that lead to the growth in the national and cosmopolitan structures. There are bound to be difficulties in achieving this goal.

Let us start with assumption that the processes are not contradictory. Of course, modernization has not succeeded in containing the process of traditionalization. It seems the two are not independent but go together. The rise of ethinicity and religious consciousness may not threaten national identities unless and until these identities claim the space and function of the structure in the national domain. In actual practice, the contradictions continue to persist. Many societies have tried to resolve this but none have succeeded so far. The European and the American models of development have led to a considerable erosion in the realm of the subject and the self with the growth of the industrial nation-state with global dimensions. And, the result is what they lament about: the erosion in family values and community life. We, in the developing societies, have to be forewarned. We have to evolve a strategy of balance in the growth of new institutions. Mechanism has to be evolved for linking up of the segmentary primordiality with the macro-structural institutions, so necessary for nation-building. For this, it is necessary to effectively implement the policies that take care of people's deprivations and disenchantments. Continued emphasis on the policies of distributive justice and social welfare that have been going on, is indispensable. Removal of illiteracy, poverty, unemployment and exploitation of the weak is essential to achieve the goals of nation-building. These will help link up the primordial with the national forces. No society can maintain itself as an integrated society unless the problems of poverty, malnutrition and empowerment of the suffering people are resolved. This linkage of the micro-structures with macro-structures may also help in the removal of the pain in the process of transition towards nation-building and industrial modernization. The problem that should worry us is as to how effective are the distributive mechanisms and policies of social and economic welfare.

The second important measure in the nation-building process is that of decentralization of power. Decentralization as a policy measure becomes increasingly essential not only to link up the micro-macro systems but also to implement social policies effectively. The recent constitutional amendment to empower village panchayats and 33 per cent reservation for women members are steps in the right direction. There is a view that the contemporary process of 'hyper modernization', with the coming of the modern computers, Internet and the cyber-space, is going to change the notion of representation as devised through elections. 'Instant polls' or 'referenda' may be possible through computers and electronic linkages. This may help in making democracy more effective and it may also empower smaller enclaves of culture and interest groups. If that happens, the notions both of the representative democracy and the decentralization of power will undergo a sea change. We may, however, debate whether this instant democrat or 'instant representation' would be a healthy process. What about the role of deliberation, or dialogue over major issues? These questions may be relevant for India in the distant future. Right now we have to examine as to how effective our institutions are that seek to decentralize power down to the grassroots. The reality is that we are at a level of polity where decentralization of power is yet to be achieved.

The third important factor in strengthening the process of nation-building is the networking of the voluntary associations. These associations increasingly play a major role in mediating between mythology and reason and between the macro-structures and the micro-structures of development. They link up different levels of social consciousness, identity and demands. The voluntary associations occupy a distinct, though complimentary, space in rendering the institutions of nation-building more meaningful to people occupying both the micro and macro domains of functioning. It is expected that such associations which will inevitably function both to promote secular cosmopolitan interests, as also those that will be anchored in religious and primordial pursuits, though distinct from one another, will work out a modality of co-existence. Even the tensions arising out of the primordial urgings may be reduced if the voluntary associations in the secular cosmopolitan sector become stronger. This will happen because the differences of subjective feelings and faith may not be able to override the commonalities of interests based on occupational and professional skills of the members. Even though members of these different associations based on common interests may come from different ethnic, religious and caste background, they do succeed in establishing a functional autonomy between primodial factors like caste, religion or ethnicity on the one hand and their professional or occupational interests on the other.

To conclude, nation-building is essentially a structural-cultural process. The distinction between structure and culture is purely heuristic. Culture is both symbolic and existential. Therefore, culture gains a dialectical quality. To view it purely as symbolic or as purely existential may lead to the "fallacy of reductionism". The process of nation-building is organically related to the successes in achieving economic and social development, distributive justice in society and the ability in society for linking 'mythology' with 'history' and 'reason'. In other words, the enclaves of culture and consciousness we define as ethnicity or local identities will have to be linked with a strategy of evolving the mediating institutions to establish complimentarities rather than contradictions between the cosmopolitan (national) and the primordial aspects of society (based on religion, ethnicity and caste).

Finally, a few words about the much debated concept of 'nation'. We should avoid a reified concept of nation on the basis of attributional parallels with other societies primarily in the West. Nation is a process, and the process of nation-building which has the flavour of 'mythology', 'history' and 'reason' is unique to each society. Our success in nation-building would depend upon the creativity and empathy that our power elite and people show in establishing convergence between pulls towards 'primordiality' and 'secularism' not only in the realm of culture but also in socio-economic development. New globalism impels us towards 'market' which is deemed as the rational paradigm of growth. But it is necessary for nation-building process, so that the metaphor of 'reason' (market) is made sensitive to the demands of welfare and social justice. The latter indeed constitutes the space which culturally sharpens consciousness of 'disenchantment'—the source of both 'history' and 'mythology'.

6

Language Legitimation and Identity

Status of Urdu and Muslims in India Since Independence

Language forms a very vital part of a nation's identity. The significance of identity in the self-perception of well-being of community has increased in importance as societies have passed from tradition to modernity and as they are now poised to enter the pathway of post-modernity. No doubt, cultural self-consciousness and sense of identity were very strong also in the traditional times. Yet, it is recognized that the intensity and pitch of the consciousness of identity could not but be self-limiting in character at this stage due to rudimentary nature of communication and production technologies. As a result of this community identities in the past had a segmentary character which could easily contain tensions of identity consciousness generated endogenously or though external contacts. The static equilibrium that traditional societies had achieved through stable nature of technologies and consequently of the production systems also constrained languages' scope for manoeuvring identities. Occupation by birth, limited space for immigration in search of employment or vocations and limited means of communication delimited the volatility of identities---whether linguistic or cultural.

The revolution in the technologies of communication and production which the modern societies have achieved and which are being rendered more acute day by day with the looming encounter with post-modernity, have altered the traditional equilibrium radically. Languages are increasingly becoming more competitive, socially and culturally differentiated and serve as an instrument of integration within the structure of economy and polity. They also constitute means of social mobility and restructuration within societies. The process of these encounters and challenges tends to render linguistic endowments of a community to become an urgent issue not only of identity but also legitimation.

LANGUAGE AND LEGITIMATION

Identities continually seek legitimation. Linguistic identity is no exception to this rule. However, identities, as they enter into the sphere of legitimation, acquire a more complex and overlapping form. The factors generally not directly contingent to language such as issues of social and economic inequalities, access to social and cultural opportunities and to power or its denial, etc., assume greater relevance. In this, the traditional conception of language as being a value-neutral phenomenon implied in most theories of linguistic-structuralism or semiotics tends to loose meaning. In the new reckoning the notion that "language forms a kind of wealth which all can make use of at once without any diminution of store, and which thus admits a complete community of enjoyment; for all freely participating in the general treasure, unconsciously aid in its preservation" as August Comte postulated, becomes redundant as it sidelines the issue of legitimation and power on an illusory assumption of linguistic communism. The fact that languages continually undergo processes of appropriation in the exercise of strategies of access to power whether symbolic, cultural or politico-economic by classes, institutions and individuals, is simply ruled out in this neutral analytical domain.

Languages, as cultural endowment, enter the arena of legitimation through their instrumental linkages with institutions such as state, market, classes and cultural values or ideologies. The state invariably intervenes through social mechanisms of play of power to designate a language as 'official' which legitimizes its entry into the category of 'legitimate language' as suggested by Pierre Bourdieu. Its role as teaching medium, its entry into school system, colleges and universities is given legitimation by political processes of the state. The state also legislates, creates and supports institutions which it recognizes as legitimate. The process through which languages are legitimated by the state for its patronage or recognition is a complex one. The mechanisms through which this is achieved are indeed not entirely political. The role of cultural and social mobilization of people's consciousness, the rise of new pressure groups, new classes or movements and the ability of some sections to appropriate the influence generated by people's linguistic mobilization, etc., influence the degree of legitimation by the state. These also usher in movements within the structure of a language to innovate upon its phonology, morphology or syntactical character. Its examples are state sponsored codification of official lexicologies, dictionaries and recognized modes of codification of languages enjoying the patronage of the state.

Market is yet another powerful institution which deeply influences the legitimation process of a language. The term 'market' can be interpreted in a narrow economic sense or in a much broader sense as an instrumental phenomenon for social and cultural allocation of resources of a people applying the laws of supply and demand or acceptance and rejection. In exceptional cases, where the state fully controls the market, the role of market in the legitimation process of language may be limited. But such situation being a rarity, it is reasonable to assume that market has through centuries served as an open-ended mechanism for introducing changes in the structure of a language, its role in society and its legitimate appropriation by classes for uses in varying contexts—economic, social, political and cultural. The elements of literary creativity, style or form in languages despite enjoying a degree of autonomy over market are subjected to its forces in substantial measure. The contemporary processes of globalization of media and capital give rise to new factors in which market forces dominate or influence the linguistic legitimation, constitution of its identity and role for the speech community.

Globalization also leads to the unification of market institutions. It imparts its own pressures on the linguistic behaviour of people from the local, regional, national to the international levels of functioning. This process generates a dual and contradictory trend in the structure and usage of language: on the one hand, it accelerates the process of 'symbolic domination' of a particular set of languages, characterized as official or legitimate, at the instrumental level, and on the other, it also enkindles sharp consciousness of the local, regional or ethnic identities. These contradictory forces, operating in the mobilization of linguistic consciousness, encourage the sense of symbolic domination of one language over others. Its bases may be varying principles of legitimacy, for example, either because the language is given legitimacy of being official or because it has greater instrumental viability for market transaction. The emerging role of the English language in the process of globalization can be one such instance. Globalization thus not only contributes to symbolic domination of an emergent language through complex mechanism of linguistic agglutination or pecking order. It also activates new awareness among people speaking languages placed lower in order of symbolic domination, such as languages spoken by minorities, local ethnic groups or those belonging to specific sub-cultures. This intense mobilization of linguistic consciousness forms a part of the celebration of their identities.

At this stage, social structural factors begin to impinge deeply upon the processes of legitimation of languages in a particular society or in the global context. Pierre Bourdieu (1991: 50-51) describes this process saying:

> "All symbolic domination presupposes, on the part of those who submit to it, a form of complicity which is neither passive submission to external constraint nor a free adherence to values. The recognition of the legitimacy of the official language has nothing in common with an explicitly professed, deliberate and revocable belief, or with an intentional act of accepting a 'norm'. It is inscribed, in a practical state, in dispositions which are impalpably inculcated, through a long and a slow process of acquisition, by the sanctions of the linguistic market, and which are, therefore, adjusted without any cynical calculation or consciously expressed constraints, to the chances of material and symbolic profit which the laws of price formation characteristic of a given market objectively offer to the holders of a given linguistic capital."

It would be simplicistic to assume that the symbolic domination of one or a set of languages is directly a result of market-governed instrumental rationality. This process is indeed a complex one, and results from people's orchestration of pre-existing linguistic orientations (which Bourdieu calls 'habitus') in stages over a period of time. The market governed impulses towards linguistic adaptation are variously rationalized depending upon the social and cultural background of the members of a specific speech community. In this context, the role of elite and middle classes assumes a great deal of significance. It is a common knowledge that members of elite and middle classes, while professing strong verbal commitment or loyalty to a language of their own community to derive political or ideological support in behaviour, deviate markedly from such norm when they send their own children to educational institutions where medium is a language of symbolic domination, e.g., Hindi or English for a Urdu speech community. Such behavioural duplicity is a universal feature of elite and middle classes in almost all marginalized speech communities. This also links the issues related to linguistic ideology with the structure of social stratification and division of classes in a speech community. Just as structure of values and general ideology are influenced by social stratification, similar processes of differentiation take place in the linguistic ideology owing to factors of social and economic inequalities within a speech community. Linguistic ideology is, therefore, subject to internal differentiation while defining people's cultural and social identity. Linguistic ideology is mobilized at two levels: general and specific. At the general level, it is externally oriented in relation to other languages outside its domain which continually orchestrate forces to emerge as a language of symbolic domination, e.g., official language, cosmopolitan language of economic and scientific transaction etc. At the specific level, linguistic ideology is oriented to deal with the internal structure and adaptive mechanisms of the language *per se* as a medium of speech, style, literary expression and power of communication. The response of a speech community to these two orientations is vitally mediated by its social structure, culture, myth, legend and history.

This point needs to be emphasized so that we recognize the fact that a community's self-consciousness about the future of its linguistic heritage cannot be understood fully in terms of a market-oriented paradigm of rationality. Factors such as history, culture, the state of collective memories improvised and continually reinforced by myths, legends and folklore, the state of internal social differentiation within the speech community, the ability to negotiate successfully between the general and specific linguistic ideologies, and finally, a community's overall perception of its future are important to comprehend the issues in totality. It is through the interplay of these complex sets of factors that language is linked with issues of identity as well as processes of legitimation.

MUSLIM COMMUNITY, IDENTITY AND URDU LANGUAGE

The analytical categories that we have employed so far are intended to help us in our understanding of the relationships between Urdu language and the issues of identity and legitimation subsisting within the Muslim community in India since independence. These analytical categories offer a theoretical framework through which a more objective comprehension of the issues can be obtained, particularly when discussions on this subject can easily drift into highly subjective or even emotive domains full of pre-existing biases. We expect that a theoretic approach can render it possible to have a more systemic and long-term appraisal of the problem, as also it may lend a certain degree of practicality to our understanding so that suitable future policies for the development of Urdu language and Muslim community in India could be formulated.

Language constituted the most vital element in the constitution of identity of any community, not to say about the Muslims in India. Its orientation and depth, as also its sharpness, is governed by a set of conditions. These are: historicity of situation in which Muslims are placed in India following partition; their socio-economic situation and their perception of opportunity profile for themselves and their children in the country in the context of their feeling of relative deprivation (in comparison with other communities); and the role of their leadership and its structure and function and the ideological and cultural movements within the community in the process of its historical evolution. All these factors, singly or in unison, influence the self-perception, subjective structure and identity of the Indian Muslims. Extensive studies are now available on most of these aspects of identity and its relationship with language for the Muslim communities in our country.

The partition following independence came as a serious blow to the Indian Muslims---both social-structurally and psychologically. A large number of elites, middle classes and entrepreneurial population migrated to Pakistan depleting the social and economic base of the community. Partition also left a sense of misplaced stigma for most Muslims living in India in the eyes of the majority community as if they were responsible for division of the country. It made most Muslims feel guilty at a time when agenda for national reconstruction and development was being drawn, the constitution was being adopted and planning process was going to set into motion. Although selectively, Muslim nationalist leadership even during this period played a key role in all these processes, and the feeling of anxiety and sense of alienation continued among the large majority of the Muslim population. During the first decade following independence Muslim identity in India could be characterized as being involuted and repressed. It was during this period that Muslim leadership was co-opted in the system to help formulate language policy. Institutional apparatuses were created to promote Urdu both as a literary heritage and as an element in the educational and administrative processes in India. Probably because of the peculiar identity crisis from which Muslims and their leadership were going through, they became acutely self-conscious in their responses to formulate and follow-up a vigorous policy for promotion of Urdu. The debate as to whether Urdu should shed its Arabic-Persian script for wider acceptability among some Muslim intellectuals is an instance which exemplifies this crisis of identity.

The quality and structure of Indian Muslim identity, however, evolved in a more equilibrated form with much self-assurance in the following decades. Several factors have contributed to this process; for example, Muslims began to regain their loss of self-confidence due to their increasing role in the electoral politics of the country; and they always moved in a significant measure from the participatory mode of state co-optation to one that was based increasingly on organizations for promotion of their language and culture. This has been particularly pronounced in the western and southern parts of India, but even in the more backward northern states the process has started gaining momentum. Muslims have, during this period, also started establishing and reviving their entrepreneurial ventures in trade, small-scale and medium-scale industries. Much of this initiative is commensurate with their traditional vocations of craftsmanship and trading. There is sign of noticeable new initiative in the field of education also in some states, particularly those in the west and south India. The emergence of Bangladesh, due to mis-management of the Bengali linguistic cultural and political identity, proved the failure of two-nation theory based on religion. This also contributed to the enrichment of Muslim identity within India. The deprivation suffered by the Urdu-speaking Mohajirs in Pakistan and those from Bangladesh may also have added impetus to the new process of identity formation.

These elements of history and sociology in evolving Muslim identity are influenced in a major part by the social structure of this community in India. Sociological studies have amply established that social and cultural inequalities, resulting from birth-ascribed caste-like institutions among the Indian Muslims, prevail almost in the same manner as among the majority of non-Muslim population. The probable exceptions are the rules of pollution and purity and social segregation. In this respect, the Muslim communities are in general more egalitarian. Nevertheless, large number of communities suffer caste-like social, economic and educational deprivations. This is proved by numerous socio-economic surveys of the Muslims conducted by the Backward Class Commission, the Minorities Commission, etc. Moreover, geographically, Muslims in India are widely dispersed. This also affects their linguistic identity. They share with other communities affiliations with languages of the region concerned. According to the Peoples of India (PoI) survey, there are 4,635 communities in whole of India, of which 534 are Muslim communities. With the exception of Arunachal Pradesh and Mizoram (where no Muslim community has been reported) all states in India have Muslim communities ranging from one each in Goa, Nagar Haveli and Sikkim to a maximum of 87 in Gujarat. Among the states having more than 30 communities include Gujarat (87), Uttar Pradesh (70), Jammu & Kashmir (59), Rajasthan (44), Bihar (41) and Delhi (30). It demonstrates the extent of social structural differentiation within the Muslim communities in India and also the level of their geographical dispersal. It also impinges deeply upon and defines the boundary of the Urdu-speaking communities among the Muslims which are concentrated in the north covering about 185 communities of Uttar Pradesh, Rajasthan, Bihar and Delhi. The PoI survey identifies communities by their spoken languages. In all 325 languages are recorded, and Urdu is spoken by 162 communities. This also includes four communities listed as scheduled castes and 158 as 'other communities'. The term 'community' is defined for the purposes of this survey as, "generally studied in ethnography which is marked by endogamy, occupation and perception" (Singh, 1992:23). Sociologically, the term 'community' as used in the PoI survey is inclusive of caste-like features. Nevertheless, there are other social formations which are not isomorphic with caste, hence the term 'community' has been preferred. To quote:

> "The first problem concerned the definition of this type of community in an all-India framework. It required a level of conceptualization that could subsume caste, non-caste structures, the minorities and those who stood outside the *varna-jati* framework. First, *jati* is an all-India word for caste; there is also the word *kulam* or *samudaya*. While caste or caste-like structures are shared by a large number of communities, there are a few communities which both ideologically and in practice deny following caste norms. Caste has weakened to some extent in recent years in terms of its adherence to hereditary occupations and norms of purity and pollution. It has also acquired new strength in a political sense as a constituency and as a vote bank. In fact, it is acquiring the characteristics an of a community as it sheds some of its traditional features. Therefore, the term 'community' or *samudaya* (as

it is called in some states like Kerala) could be a more appropriate concept for an all-India reference than caste with its various local names" (Singh, 1992: 23-24).

The above definitional clarification of the notion of community being a caste-like social organization identified through hereditary occupations which has now weakened a great deal is the predominant phenomenon. It is quite arguable to infer that Muslims segmented as they are through 584 communities equally share with the rest of the Indian population comparable degree of social differentiation and status hierarchy based on occupational and endogamous exclusiveness. The imprint of this feature on ideology and identity can be indeed remarkable. The PoI survey notes that nomenclature of most communities in India follows secular categories and only "about three per cent derived their name from religious affiliation such as Adi-dharmi, Ahmadiya, Aradhyulu etc..." Nevertheless one should not be oblivious of the significance of religious and cultural factors in the location of identity of the Muslim communities in India in general.

However, the importance of social stratification and inequalities among Muslims within and in relation to the non-Muslim communities cannot be overlooked in the context of their self-perception defending their cultural and social identity. The partition had depleted the Muslim community of a major segment of the middle classes, elites, professionals and enterprising sections. However, during the past five decades since independence, the process of social and economic development has bridged this gap to some extent. Yet, it remains uneven and regionalist. In the western and southern India, sections of Muslims have progressed in trade, commerce and small-scale industries. Their level of education is also much better. The economic and social rehabilitation of Muslims have been most problematic in the northern states of Bihar, Uttar Pradesh, Madhya Pradesh and Rajasthan where majority of their population is concentrated. In these states, little social mobility has taken place among Muslims, a very small segment of the middle class has emerged in the midst of a mass of backward Muslim population. Some studies suggest that a new emotional and political cleavage is taking place between the Muslim elites and Muslim dalits and backwards in many northern states. A sense of disenchantment among the Muslim masses who remain poor and backward is also growing. They feel that elites, both Muslim and non-Muslim, use them only as vote-banks without taking concrete measures for their social and economic advancement. The demand for affirmative action by the government in their favour is gaining wider support.

A similar feeling of relative deprivation also prevails among the Muslim middle classes. Their representation in government jobs, professional positions and in assemblies and parliament remains widely disproportionate to their population. Rafiq Zakaria, in a study, has brought out such anomalies in telling terms. He writes: "Muslims form 12 per cent of the population of India. In the general elections to Lok Sabha held recently 20 states including Maharashtra, Punjab, Orissa, Rajasthan and Tamilnadu did not elect a single Muslim, nor did any Union Territory (except Lakshadweep which is entirely Muslim). Their 12 per cent of population should have given them over 60 seats: only 28 Muslims were returned to the 12th Lok Sabha. ...Muslim employment in government services and public sector enterprises presents an even more dismal picture: engineers 2 per cent, doctors 2.5 per cent, IAS 2.86 per cent, ITOs 3.01 per cent, Class I officers 3.3 per cent, bank employees 2.18 per cent. Muslim representation in private enterprises is marginally higher than in government controlled organizations----4.08 per cent" (cited in Singh, 1998) There are complex set of factors which explain such a low level of representation. A similar sense of relative deprivations is also witnessed among the backward class non-Muslims but admittedly the problem is more acute in the case of Muslims in general. There is a strong case for addressing this problem educationally and socially. This feeling of relative deprivation among the Muslims no doubt influences the structure and orientation of their identity.

The resurgence of movements to strengthen cultural and religious identities or to constitute Muslim identity only through their cultural and religious exclusiveness is a product of the perception and reality of their social and economic deprivation. Urdu language has over the years assumed a very significant space in the structure of Muslim identity in India. It no longer remains confined as an elite sub-culture of literary and courtly style. Its aristocratic antecedents have now given way to a degree of homogenization of not so much of its style but its linguistic uses and its institutional face which pervade among Muslims in almost all parts of India. It forms a part of their cultural identity. Over the decades following independence, the class barriers and distinctive stylization in the uses of the Urdu language have given way to a perception among Muslims that this language articulates their religious, cultural and civilizational identity. Its market orientation has in this process weakened along with its administrative patronage. The issue of cultural identity has thus appropriated the maximum space of legitimacy in respect of this language. This should engage our attention as we seek to enlarge its space of legitimation through its access to market, administrative and inter-cultural discourse.

As a consequence of these new changes in the identity-related dimensions of the Urdu language, earlier acceptability of this language across religious and cultural divides has narrowed. Its older cosmopolitan attraction for many non-Muslim middle classes in northern India and the Deccan no longer exists as in the past. No doubt, this attraction was not entirely due to the literary and cultural excellence of Urdu. It was also for reasons of its administrative patronage and marketability. Urdu language endowed people access to administration and a range of job opportunities controlled by the state and the feudal nobility. A major change has taken place after independence in the Muslim community's response to the Urdu language. It is now increasingly confined to a role that serves to reinforce Muslim cultural, social and religious identities. Consequently, its systemic alienation from the mainstream processes of education, administration and market mechanisms has taken place. Moreover, the absence of a strong and well-networked institutional system among Muslims, which may promote Urdu and contribute to its pedagogic modernization across the country on voluntary basis, has blocked its growth. The extent of social and economic backwardness of the Muslims, together with the lack of their political empowerment, has only compounded this limitation.

EDUCATIONAL BACKWARDNESS OF THE MUSLIMS

Sociology of development has now adequately established a close causal relationship between the level of literacy and education in a community and the quality and rate of its development. With a few exception in the southern states of India, the Muslims lag behind in education relative to other communities in India. This is despite the general educational backwardness in our country. Even though the gross literacy level has moved up, about half of the Indian population is illiterate and literacy is abysmally low (in some north Indian states as low as 90 per cent) among the females. In this scenario of our failure after 50 years of independence, the position of the Muslim community is relatively worse. Studies of educational levels of the Muslims in India conducted by several scholars have confirmed this. According to the Planning Commission survey of 1987-88, "the national literacy rate was approximately 52 per cent, while for Muslims it was 42 per cent. There is a marked disparity between Hindus and Muslims in respect of education. The percentage of Hindus who have completed high school is 3.4, while for Muslims it is 1.2. The percentage of graduates among Hindus is 7.9 whereas for Muslims it is 2.3. The drop-out rate is quite high among Muslims. On an average, about one-third of literates among Muslims drop out before attaining the requisite level. The highest drop-out rate is observed at the middle level. The drop-out in the 20-24 years age group is as high as 50 per cent. Gender disparity in respect of literacy among Muslims is appalling. The literacy rate for Muslim women is 34 per cent. Only one per cent of Muslim women reach high school. Haryana has reported total illiteracy for Muslim women. At the all-India level, Muslim women are three-times behind their Hindu sisters. The attainment of higher education among girls is a rare phenomenon even in the urban areas" (Manzoor Alam, 1998:10-11).

This educational backwardness of Muslims goes together with their economic backwardness for whose developmental policies of the state and central governments have not succeeded so far. Studies conducted by the Planning Commission, and other agencies such as National Sample Survey, National Council of Applied Economic Research, Minorities Commission, etc., consistently confirm this situation. Muslims exist at the neglected end of the spectra of communities of India in social, economic and political field and the overall process of empowerment. Their political representation in assemblies and parliament has been declining in spite of the fact that "there are 14 districts in India with a Muslim majority and 114 districts where the Muslim population is 15 per cent and above. There are 120 parliamentary and 700 assembly constituencies all over the country in which Muslim votes are a decisive factor in the elections. Compare it to the 5.9 per cent Muslim representation (28 members) in the 12th Lok Sabha. The highest percentage was 8.50 in 1980 (46 members). In Uttar Pradesh, the number of Muslims elected to Lok Sabha has fallen from 17 in 1991 to just 6 in 1998 in spite of the fact that Muslims constitute 22 per cent of the states population" (Manzoor Alam, 1998:13). Whatever the reasons for this disproportionately low level of political representation---may be faulty electoral process or the nature of political mobilization or alliances or an electoral system which calls for reform---the phenomenon of lack of political empowerment has deeply fractured the nature of Muslim identity. The issue of language as an element in Muslim identity is reinforced by their feeling of general relative deprivation. Identity being a complex and composite phenomenon, the perceptions of Muslims about the present neglect and decline of Urdu is bound to constitute an organic element in the formation of their collective identity.

THE STATE OF THE URDU LANGUAGE AND POLICY

The historicity of partition and the psychology it generated has deeply influenced the state's Urdu language policy after independence. The issue has been viewed by political actors and the majority community from an emotive and communal perspective. One could easily discern the shadow of these factors overwhelming the responses which deliberated state policy. A major element in the new situation also emanated from the democratic process itself. It had to reconcile with public opinion regarding language policy. Its orientation towards Urdu was iniquitous in comparison with the status that this language enjoyed during the British rule. Urdu was marginalized in the affairs of the state and administration. In the educational system, as a factor in curricula or as a medium of teaching and research, Urdu was trapped into a three-language formula which never quite took off. In operational terms, the three-language formula was applied in a manner discriminatory to Urdu. The formula left options open by which Urdu could be institutionally by-passed. In policy implementation, despite positive intentions it turned out to be a sham. Urdu was accorded the 'official' status as a language by states without integrating it with vital institutions of education, educational processes or administration. A large number of institutions, panels, commissions and academies were created to promote the cause of Urdu language which did not succeed. Instead, state sponsored institutions, academies and National Council for Promotion of Urdu (erstwhile Urdu Promotion Bureau) created a perception among the large masses of Muslim population as being strategies to play self-serving co-optational politics within the leadership structure of the Muslim community. These institutions neither made a meaningful impact nor enjoyed legitimacy or credibility among the Urdu speech community which got increasingly localized among the Muslim community.

The crisis confronting Urdu is an outcome of the failure of the state to implement the language policy at the primary and secondary levels of education. Its effective role could ensure that Urdu speech community had a sizeable student population to join colleges and universities to pursue higher level studies of Urdu language and literature and as effective medium to study other subjects with proficiency. Without such back-up from students graduating through high school or secondary level education enrolment of students in the Urdu Departments in colleges and universities has shrunk forcing them to waive the requirement of having learnt Urdu for university level studies in the subject. This policy had two negative consequences for the growth of Urdu: first, delinking of Urdu qualification as prerequisite for higher studies took away the pressure from the state governments to effectively implement the policy of teaching Urdu at the primary and secondary levels, and secondly, it produced undergraduates and graduate with degrees in Urdu language who in most cases were below standard. This substandard population of Urdu graduates increasingly perpetuates a vicious cycle of deteriorating standards of Urdu teaching and research.

It may be necessary to posit this problem in relation to the responses of educated Muslim elite, litterateurs and college and university teachers in a wider context. Historicity of changing identity situations and legitimacy of Urdu as perceived by Muslim elite and middle classes during 1950s and 1960s played a significant role. We have discussed some of the socio-historical factors which confounded the future prospect of Urdu. Given these factors, the choices that Muslim intellectuals in colleges and universities had to make about admission policy was indeed critical without an alternate solutions in sight. Without mobilization of people's consciousness and institutional support for Urdu, the precarious compromise made at the university level teaching of Urdu is self-explanatory. It must be realized that following partition, the major institutional anchorages on which the stability of Urdu language was based, totally broke down. The support of the state, and the market prospects of this language were deeply affected. The crisis of ideology, on the other hand, and the defensive attitude of the Muslim elite and middle classes, rendered the support for Urdu more ineffective.

GROWTH OF URDU LANGUAGE SINCE INDEPENDENCE

One could not possibly evaluate the growth of Urdu in India, either substantively or normatively, without defining the term 'growth'. As we have outlined in our conceptual enunciation, a language can be seen to have achieved a high growth trajectory if it enjoyed institutional support from authorities (governments, public bodies), was well integrated with the market forces linked to production and communication processes, created intellectual products of high quality, generated skills through rational human resource development, was supported by not only the speech community but also elite and middle classes; finally it was also necessary that possibility existed to orchestrate all these factors into a coherent cultural and ideological policy. These factors together define the optimum condition which language must enjoy to reach a credible level of legitimation. It could then inculcate a sense of confidence among the speech community in a world where languages—local, national and cosmopolitan—are fiercely competing for 'symbolic domination'.

Unfortunately, a systematic study of languages in India, of which Urdu is no exception using analytical parameters as outlined, has not been conducted. Yet, it is possible to arrive at some conclusions about the trends of development of Urdu in the country since independence. A survey of four representative states (Bihar, Andhra Pradesh, Maharashtra and West Bengal conducted by Athar Farouqui, gives us a picture of the trends in the education of Urdu in the light of state policies, particularly "three languages formula" enunciated in the resolution on National Policy on Education and modified in 1975 by the Gujaral Committee. The impact of these policies on the promotion of Urdu has obviously been disappointing mainly because of loopholes provided in the policy to escape teaching Urdu or using it as a medium of instruction wherever possible. In Uttar Pradesh alone, the condition of Urdu education is reported to be most pathetic. "There is not even a single primary or junior high school of Urdu medium. The only two Urdu medium high schools are those run by and affiliated to Aligarh Muslim University. During the last decade there has been a mushroom growth of private schools everywhere in the state. This has given rise to several complexities in the field of education. About 50 to 60 per cent of these schools are unrecognized. Still the middle and lower middle class people opt to send their children to these schools for education, even though it is very well known that these institutions are merely business centres" (Farouqui, 1994:781). These schools teach only upto fifth standard being non-recognized and students have to move up to recognized schools for further studies which involves effort and expenses. The state of Uttar Pradesh does offer students choices of studying subjects through Urdu medium, but under this scheme, the desired choice of optional subjects is not made available which discourages students.

The state also offers option of appearing for junior high school examination with Urdu as medium, but the number of such students is very small. This number was below 500 in 1982 as compared to nearly 40,000 in Bihar in the same year. Constraint is such that Muslim students prefer Hindi medium as it helps them in higher studies of their choice and in employment.

New schemes introduced for teaching through Urdu medium introduced by late H.N. Bahuguna have not made desired progress due to lack of motivation and qualified teachers. Bihar has comparatively done better. It may be because of the self-help policy pursued there by the Muslim community. Urdu teaching here is integrated with religious institutions through sacred texts. Madarasas have proliferated with massive support from the Muslim lower and lower middle classes. Perception is that the class support for Urdu in Bihar is qualitatively different in comparison with Uttar Pradesh. "Every year in Bihar", writes Farouqui, "60,000 students take junior high school and high school examinations is recognized by the Bihar government as equivalent to other recognized Boards. Effort is on to introduce science and technology (vocational) courses in these schools. A major problem they face is of shortage of standard textbooks in Urdu language. The absence of rational management practices in the Madarasa Educational Board are also held responsible for thwarting progress in the desired direction. Formulation of new courses and upgradation of their content is acutely required."

In western India, Maharashtra has come out more successful in the promotion of Urdu education. This is largely because of private and voluntary initiatives launched by individual businessmen and trusts which run and manage Urdu medium schools efficiently. Teaching is conducted with regularity and emphasis remains on merit. Mumbai city alone has 124 registered Urdu medium high schools, whereas there are 230 registered Urdu medium high schools in the whole of Maharashtra. The state government has also been cooperative and helpful in promoting Urdu in Maharashtra. The middle class Muslims encourage their children to study in Urdu medium schools only because of their good standard. Probably, the predominance of the business ethos among the Muslims in this region oriented to mercantile values has helped Muslim cultural self-awareness to promote Urdu not only as a modern subject but also as a means to promote cultural heritage. Urdu, as an optional subject, is now available at colleges and higher level educational institutions. Several convent schools also offer facilities of teaching Urdu. All in all, Maharashtra offers a model of how education through voluntary effort and state cooperation can be promoted with good results.

In south India, Andhra Pradesh offers yet another example of Urdu education. For centuries Deccan has been one of the major centres of Urdu literature and learning. Hyderabad, after Delhi and Lucknow, occupied a place of utmost eminence in promoting and sponsoring literary creativity in Urdu along with specific contributions to augmenting its linguistic style and sophistry. Before partition, Urdu enjoyed both political patronage and elite support in this region. Osmania University in Hyderabad State (before reorganization) used to employ Urdu medium for higher education including teaching of engineering and medicine. But, in today's Andhra Pradesh, Urdu does not seem to be faring well. "Urdu is moving fast towards its imminent death in Hyderabad", writes Farouqui.

Most Urdu learning is confined either to Madarasas or to schools run on voluntary basis. The drop-out rate in these schools is very high running upto 40 per cent between class one and ninth and touches 43 per cent at high school level. In terms of class support, even the lower middle classes in Hyderabad do not strongly patronize Urdu medium schools.

These trends of Urdu education in the state have significant bearing upon future policy about the promotion of Urdu language and literature and preservation of its cultural identity. There is need for integrating Urdu education with forces of modernization such as marketability, contribution to science and technology and holistic cultural development. As witnessed, the role of state with few exceptions seems to run into serious self-limiting conditions on the questions of promotion of Urdu. The counter-pulls of vote-banks in the democratic process, backwardness of the Muslim community and absence of strong mobilization of Muslim community for the cause of

Urdu renders the response of states in India rather half-hearted or even pretentious in extending institutional and financial support on the desired scale. Hence, the centrality of the role of private and voluntary efforts from within the Muslim community to take charge of the initiative goes without saying. The extent to which such mobilization may succeed depends upon the nature of identity formation, cultural self-consciousness, social and economic mobility and political empowerment of Muslim community in India.

Urdu developed as a language of literary depth, style and sub-culture due to its linkages with such traditional institutions as the camp, the court and the bazar (market). A qualitative change has now taken place in all these institutions due to the process of modernization. The camp and the court have been replaced by the modern democratic state which in day-to-day functioning is guided by pressure groups and interest group politics. After the reorganization of the states on linguistic lines soon after independence, Urdu not having a territorial viability was accorded official recognition but lost its political punch. This together with fluctuations in the nature of identity formation of the Muslim community following partition failed to create conducive situation for the cause of Urdu. A set of new social and psychological forces came into play in the subjective and objective perceptions of Urdu as a linguistic heritage which further confounded its growth leading to the marginalization of Urdu language and literature in independent India.

A study by Farouqui 200 scholars on various aspects of the future of Urdu in India and reasons for its inadequate pace of development brings out interesting results. Most scholars continue to view Urdu language and literature as a part of composite Indian culture shared both by Muslims and non-Muslims. They do not associate Urdu either exclusively with Islam or with Muslim community. They are also not prepared to posit antinomy between Urdu and Hindi as they feel that both these languages are sister languages and product of peculiar

Indian historicity and its secular tradition. For slow momentum in growth of Urdu they blame promoters' overdependence on government. The degree of indifference among Muslims to teach their children through Urdu medium, and of their patronage to Urdu literature, newspapers and magazines, is also seen as a factor inhibiting growth of Urdu. Obviously, most Urdu literates continue to espouse a secular perspective on the substantive character of the Urdu language and literature. However, the changing ground realities and the pattern of growth of Urdu education is pulling it fast into an exclusivist Islamic domain. The changing social structural forces both within the Muslim community and outside may partly explain this process. But luke-warm state policy in respect of Urdu education seen through a communal tint holds major responsibility for the present trend towards de-secularization of Urdu teaching.

In the absence of incorporation of Urdu teaching into the composite structures of teaching institutions, schools and colleges, it is the Madarsas under the leadership of grassroots Muslim traders, artisans and peasants belonging to the lower-middle classes, where the initiative has shifted. Here, religious cannonization overarchs the ethos of education. Thus, a strong linkage between religion and education is established which may essentially not be undesirable if such teaching could be integrated with modern values and skills in education. Much reform is needed in this area as the evaluation of curricula and textbooks under use in the Madarsa schools suggests.

Urdu language's exclusivist identification with Muslim community has no doubt increased during the past fifty years despite intellectuals continued faith in its secular and composite cultural character. This is because of the indifferent manner in which policies for the promotion of Urdu education have been articulated and implemented by various states and also by the Muslim leadership whose focus has been to save Urdu as a means to promote cultural-religious heritage rather than as an instrument of modernization. The Madarasas have today given

Urdu education, language and literature an exclusivist orientation enmeshed within the Muslim religious-cultural identity. Hence, several issues in the future policy formulation for the promotion of Urdu language and literature arise. One of them, as discussed in the following section, is how to establish linkages between Urdu education and the emergent market phenomenon in our country and abroad.

URDU EDUCATION, COMMUNICATION AND MARKET

Traditionally, Urdu arose with a closer linkage with the bazar (market). It did enjoy patronage of the ruling political and cultural elite but was not alienated from utilization of market ethos. The market for Urdu educated graduates was available in teaching jobs, civil, judicial and revenue services, management of the estates of the feudal nobility and job opportunities in courts which organized cultural activities. This system reached its peak during the medieval period and continued with some changes throughout the British rule in India. Following independence and partition of the country major changes were introduced in economy, social structure and educational policies which placed Urdu education and its market relationship into an entirely new environment. It was marginalized from most of the earlier institutional linkages. Market for Urdu graduates began to shrink and its scope became narrower and confined to few available teaching jobs only. Much later, job opportunities in media and communication have become available, but it depends upon the growth of Urdu press, publication industry and broadcasting media. We need to meticulously analyze the interface between Urdu education and dimensions of its marketability in order to evolve policies that add vigour to the processes of economic and social modernization of the Muslim community.

Independence radically changed the character of the institutions which traditionally patronized Urdu language and education. The traditional bazar, which was essentially anchored on the feudal-mercantile economy with artisan mode of production, was pushed into industrial ambience of development. It is now increasingly being overwhelmed by predominance of new services sector of economy. The nature of court, as existent in the medieval and colonial period, had been structurally replaced. A few of its earlier features may still survive but are generally deligitimated. The institution of feudalism and its social and cultural bases have been abolished. The nation is going through a rapid though painful process of two revolutions: liberal-democratic and industrial-technological. These developments have caused a legitimation crises for many traditional cultural and social institutions, and most of them are now undergoing fast adaptive changes to integrate with evolving new realities. Language and education are no exception to this process.

In any future planning for growth of Urdu education, significance of linkages with market and economy would have to play a key role. Globalization of economy and technology with enormous backing from communication and media revolution creates a unique situation offering scope for synergy between language and market. It augments the capacity of a language to extend and intensify its cultural and economic roles within the country and beyond. The rate of migration between societies is so accelerated that it creates strong cultural and linguistic diaspora of communities on a global scale. The production of services far surpasses the commodity production in economy. Workforce engaged in telecommunication, journalism, media advertising, health care, teaching and dissemination of symbols or cultural products, etc., dominates the occupational profile. Trade, banking, insurance, transportation, management and production of skills reinforce the role of services in the new industrial society. All this makes a significant and qualitative difference in the structure and function of capitalism and industrialism. Super-skilled and vocationalized labour and not manual labour are required in abundance. Quick turnover in technology and shifting grounds of capital-investment flows at a global level preordain continual upgradation of skills. Occupational profile of an individual ceases to have lifetime tenure, redundancy of jobs may become endemic and learning of new skills a necessity. Education process for meeting the challenges of such a future society requires intimate market linkages.

Education and information play a determinate role in defining the market situation for individuals in search of employment. The neo-capitalist and post-industrial economy not only globalizes and homogenizes cultures and consumption patterns, but also creates enclaves of local cultures and sub-cultures globally through expansion of ethnic and linguistic diaspora, intensification of communication-culture linkages by information technologies of telephony and Internet. Thus, even a minority or local linguistic group may enjoy market viability, particularly in the domains of culture, journalism, communication and commerce if it modernizes its paradigm. Urdu can be no exception to this process.

The new phase of economic development not only alters the market situation for languages externally (outside the country) but also within the society. The crucial factors which govern the viability of a language for the internal market are: modernization of teaching in the language and its orientation to services and the integrative capacity within the linguistic community to absorb in its educational system the skills and vocations that the emergent new economies may require. The responses to these new demands in education influence the market prospect of a language. For instance, the literacy level of a community has direct implication to potential for print media circulation in a specific language. The role of press, radio, television and other modes of communication in the promotion of culture and generation of skills in Urdu language has been slow not only because of the faulty policies of the state but also because of relatively lower levels of literacy and education in the

Muslim community.

The growth of Urdu journalism and press has not been commensurate with general expectations of the Muslim community. The total number of the Urdu newspapers and periodicals does not reveal their real status in terms of actual circulation. According to the Ministry of Information & Broadcasting figures, in 1992, there were 347 newspapers/periodicals registered, of which only 50 were reaching the public. Studies also show that a steep decline in circulation took place soon after partition. However, a little improvement was discerned in 1980s when some daily newspapers were launched and a few which had ceased publication were revived. Compared to dailies, the weekly publications command wider readership and have good circulation. Yet, the readership is still limited and the members belonging to the upper middle segment of the population do not give it enough patronage. The south Indian Muslim community runs its own publications in regional medium even though the reach of the Urdu press has now increased. The state-controlled media, such as the radio and television, have slots for Urdu programme broadcasting/telecasting. The radio has in this respect given a better account of itself than the television. The tolerance for programmes telecast in Urdu runs on communal lines. The problem is also caused by adhocism in scheduling of such programmes. A comprehensive and well integrated policy in this area needs to be evolved in consultation with community leaders of major religious groups.

The significance of vigorous and objective Urdu press and publication of literature in Urdu lies not only in its value for enlarging the scope of market for Urdu graduates. It will also offer a reliable and credible channel of communication within the Muslim community to impart balanced and responsible information about events, socio-economic and cultural developments and formation of integrative and balanced viewpoint on relevant issues. Studies have shown that press not only serves as a channel for information but also as an instrument for construction of realities. In certain situations of communal conflicts, the role of press becomes most sensitive. Comparative studies of cosmopolitan press and vernacular press have shown that vernacular press tends to suffer from biases in reporting events and interpreting the same through lead articles and editorials. The national (English medium) press has given a better account of itself in this regard. There is scope for reforms in Urdu press. But, the Hindi press and press in other regional languages deserve our closer attention in this regard.

In a plural and democratic society, such as ours, ideological differences are bound to exist. So also contradictions of interests in social, economic and cultural fields. Press has enormous responsibility to serve as not only a medium of communication of events and viewpoints in a balanced and constructive manner, but also a means for articulation of people's cultural symbols and aspirations embedded in the structure of people's identity. Press, therefore, serves as a major tool for empowerment and legitimation of identity. This is true for all ethnic groups. So also for the Muslims in India, with a population of more than 120 million. Press has to evolve an active and integrated institutional set-up not only to promote Urdu education but also to act as a reliable and responsible mediating instrument of communication and information. This is particularly relevant because of the wide-spread feeling among the Muslims that press in general has not fully empathized with their social, economic, political and cultural concerns.

The press and the electronic media such as radio, television, telephony, Internet, fax, e-mail, etc., introduced new vistas in management of information and ideology in our society. Such developments, as the evidence from more developed countries suggests, are deeply influencing or even redefining the role of state, market, class and culture. These lead to a great deal of obsolescence of myriad of existing and pre-existing controls. The press is going to face great pressure in respect of its technology, management and marketing. Communication revolution taking place today is bound to enhance the autonomy of small and marginalized communities all over the world. It will help preserve their identities. Hence, the communication revolution may not only bring about cultural homogenization but it may further reinforce identities of plural cultures and sub-cultures. All these advantages may accrue to communities with higher educational endowment. Muslims in India on this count suffer from greater degree of relative deprivation.

Both Urdu education and Urdu press have shown better results in the regions where entrepreneurial level of educated Muslims is higher. It gives them greater initiative to launch and support Urdu press. This happens even though the percentage of Urdu-knowing population may not be large but the sense of cultural identity is strong. Farouqui (1995:101) in a study reports: "The state of Urdu journalism is far more favourable in those linguistic regions of India where Muslims are proud of their identity and are actively sharing the region's cultural ethos. In all such regions the percentage of the population that knows Urdu is much smaller than in north India. Even in those regions where Urdu is not the mother tongue of Muslims the situation of Urdu is much better than in north India, and the attitude of Muslims towards Urdu is pragmatic not emotional". It may be added that relative advancement of the Muslims in the southern and western regions of India in economic and educational fields has given them innate social and cultural strength to articulate identity in a self-assured manner. Studies have consistently shown a positive correlation between levels of economic and educational development of a community and the maturity of its cultural and social self-awareness.

LEGITIMATION AND SYMBOLIC DOMINATION

A major loss to the Urdu language during the past fifty years is its displacement as a language of symbolic domination. Paradoxically, the more its acceptability has become exclusive to the

Muslim community and the more it has been perceived as a linguistic and cultural heritage of the Muslims alone, the more it has been alienated from the composite cultural stream which was its main integrative strength. In recent years Urdu has gained greater cultural space among Muslims which adds vigour to its symbolic domination within this community. At the national level or across cultures, it has lost its significance as a language of symbolic domination. A distinction needs to be made between concepts of cultural domination and symbolic domination. Cultural domination, in sociological term, implies depth of support in a certain community for accepting the legitimacy of a culture trait such as language in our case. Symbolic domination, on the other hand, means the degree of prestige accorded to the same culture trait within the community or outside. Major changes in the policy of states towards Urdu language have adversely affected its market value; the apathy of the upper and the middle class Muslims towards Urdu and the tendency in the Muslims community to appropriate it merely as a religious-cultural phenomenon have reduced its utilitarian as well as ideological appeal. It no longer is being patronized by the state, or the market as in the past. The job opportunities for its graduates have become negligible but for a limited number of teaching positions. All this signifies the loss of symbolic domination of Urdu language.

The need is to restore in credible measure its lost position in the process of symbolic domination. This would require radical restructuring of the policies for its future growth. There is also need for attitudinal changes among the Muslims to broaden the instrumental and cultural significance of Urdu as a heritage not only of their community but of the nation as a whole. The contradiction between the cultural versus symbolic aspects of domination in case of Urdu language equally applies to other Indian languages including Hindi. These languages, which enjoy considerable state patronage and articulate higher degree of cultural domination in the social space, also painfully realize erosion in their symbolic domination as a result of ascendance of English. This results from their precarious linkages with the market, now in the process of economic globalization. Regional languages are under pressure to engage in interaction with other regional languages and with English having a cosmopolitan status. This happens due to enormous growth in volume and scope of communication, greater inter-cultural, inter-regional and inter-national contacts, higher incidence of migration between regions in the country and outside. One result is increase in bilingualism and the other increased creolization of languages in various usages. There is uninhibited assimilation of vocabulary drawn from inter-regional and cosmopolitan linguistic contacts. The pressure from market is constantly increasing in scope and significance. In this context, each Indian language would have to reorient policy of self-growth. This equally applies to Urdu which suffers from double handicaps; first, from crisis of legitimacy and increased loss of symbolic domination in comparison to other regional languages, and secondly, the indifference of state authorities and administration about augmenting the process of its growth.

Our analysis suggests that for promotion of Urdu language and its education a systematic policy needs to be evolved. It should be sensitive to all factors responsible for its present state of alienation. It would take into account the reasons responsible for continual failure of the state policies for promotion of Urdu. It should include the measures for increasing its marketability and its techno-managerial utility. Steps must be taken to modernize Urdu education, to elecit Muslim elite and middle classes interest for active support for this language. The Muslim leadership has to exercise a large measure of autonomy, and policy of self-help has to be promoted through democratic movements for the promotion of Urdu education. A democratic polity responds to the rights of a community sympathetically depending upon the degree of community mobilization for redresasal of its demands. It is possible that in case of the Urdu education there has been some vacillation in projection of demand by the Muslim elite and middle classes. The leadership role for promotion of Urdu performed by leaders coming from the lower middle and lower classes of the Muslim community has tended to be self-limiting. Their efforts have no doubt served the cause of Urdu education. But, due to their narrow ideological perspective mainly confined to religious-cultural values such as in Madarsa paradigm of education its linkages with modernization, have by-passed the process of growth. Thus, there is need for effort by the Muslim community to incorporate element of modern techno-scientific learning and skill in a new paradigm of Urdu education. It would help in enlarging the scope of its legitimation as also its position as a language of symbolic domination.

ETHNICIZATION OF MUSLIM COMMUNITY AND URDU EDUCATION

The above analysis is based mainly on application of two sociological categories, viz., community and ethnicity, to explain the contemporary linguistic movements not only in India but all over the world. Increasingly, communities are being ethnicized. The network of social and cultural relationships which traditionally a community nourished in India allowed space for cultural and social interaction with other communities. It is now being replaced by segmentary religious and cultural relationships. Increasing cultural self-consciousness is turned into ethnicity, generates ethnic movement and is politicized. Ethnicization process evolves primarily from politicization of cultural and existential self-images of a community. The process of ethnicization results into revival and recreation of myths, legends and images on which new identities are founded. Both the Muslim and the Hindu communities in India have been extensively going through this process. The root of communal politics in India is entrenched in such a soil.

Though ethnicization of the Muslim community has recently accelerated in pace, it has a long history. Earlier, the community even though maintaining its identity, continued to share many regional, social and cultural traditions with most other non-Muslim communities. The legitimation of this composite culture though weakening continues to remain valid due to the historicity and plurality of Indian regional and local cultures and social formation overarched by civilizational convergence as they are. No doubt, many influential leaders and parties, both among the Hindus and Muslims attempt to culturally segmentalize ethnicity even though the civilizational bonds across religions remain strong in India. Even the contemporary social reality of various communities across religious divide in India does not support isolationist ethnicization. The PoI survey using the measure of 776 cultural traits (trait being "treated as cultural value, which is unique") had found that the correlation of traits between the Hindus and Muslims (which) is very high indeed. It adds: "Communities also share traits in terms of food habits, material culture, folklore, etc. There is also an all-pervasive sense of reverence for the sacred and for life. The little traditions blend with Islam and other organized religions at the folk level. Almost all communities throng the sacred shrines associated with pirs etc." (1992:99). This cultural commonality continues to subsist along with distinct social and cultural traits specific to each community or religion. Increasingly, the role of politics and quest for a share in power have assumed greater role in ethnicization of religious communities necessitating new policy responses.

Nevertheless, ethnicization as a cultural process has a vital role to play in the developmental strategies of Urdu language in India. To a large extent, Urdu has been a victim of this process. The halting and half-hearted policies of many states, particularly Uttar Pradesh, bear testimony to this fact. More importantly, ethnicization when it takes emotional overtones or when its agenda is defined by narrow segmentary articulation of cultural values which seemingly conflict with other cultures, leads to communal conflict. This obstructs the process of formulating realistic and objective policies and their appraisal. The two processes once begun form a vicious cycle. Not only state, but voluntary promotional efforts by Muslims also for the growth of Urdu language sometimes suffer from its influence. The Madarsa paradigm of Urdu education can be one such instance.

Should we conclude that ethnicization process of Muslim (also other communities) community in India necessarily obstructs development of Urdu education? The answer is clearly negative. Our review of development of Urdu education since independence indicates that most promotional activities for Urdu education have come from the internal resources mobilized by the Muslim community. This effort has coincided with increasing sensitivity of Muslims to the cultural and religious identity. This process is also linked with social mobility among Muslims, such as the rise of entrepreneurial and mercantile classes, surpluses generated from Muslim diaspora and some improvement in the economic condition of Muslims over the past five decades. The fact that such mobility has been more in the western and peninsular India than in the northern states, is illustrative of the strong relationship between educational growth and social development. The reservation policy of southern states has also been helpful for Muslims. Urdu education in this region also has more modern orientation. The nature of economic and educational growth of Muslims impinges deeply upon the pattern of their ethnicization, as to whether it is segmentary or promotes such cultural and religious autonomy with sharing cultural and social linkages with communities outside, contextualized in a cosmopolitan framework of values and interests, essential for a liberal democracy. To achieve this, economic and educational development of Muslims is essential. This will contribute to integrated growth of the larger Indian society and polity.

TOWARDS A PARADIGM

Let us now recapitulate the issues that we have raised in our discussion of identity, legitimacy and its relationship with Urdu education. Clearly, the past fifty years have witnessed an evolution of the cultural identity of the Muslim community. Its direction, where voluntary efforts with economic development have been higher, has more empathy for cultural pluralism, liberal democracy and social and economic modernization. There exist, however, some pockets of segmentary ethnicization of the community. It is linked with the perception of Muslims, often legitimate, that state's economic and educational policies have either not been fairly implemented or have not followed the principle of equity to deal with problems of Muslim backwardness in our society. There also exists a relationship between positive or negative pattern of ethnicization of Muslims in India and the level of their social, economic and educational development.

The reality and perception of state's lukewarm response to formulating and implementing effective action plan for promotion of Urdu education, a constitutional covenant for the Indian State, has led to considerable degree of alienation of the Muslim community. The voluntary efforts by the community for promotion of Urdu has proved more effective to achieve the goal. Its negative fall-out is that Urdu has increasingly lost its link with the paradigm of a composite culture, hugely celebrated and idealized since independence. It has become isomorphic to an exclusivist Muslim cultural repertoire. This weakens Muslim community's confidence in the legitimacy of state policies which profess to idealize composite culture. The state, both at the Centre and in provinces, needs to recognize this problem. This should help in reorientation of policies and their implementation.

A second set of issues vital for the growth of Urdu education concerns the initiative of the Muslim community itself. It seems that the Muslim elite and middle classes have not come forward to share the responsibility to make organized voluntary effort for the modernization of Urdu education. The examples of such effort already available are limited in nature. There is need to mobilize the community and its leadership to promote Urdu education in a comprehensive manner with financial, professional and cultural mobilization of resources now available within Muslim community. Such voluntary effort with social and cultural mobilization should be integrated with institutional and political movement for Urdu education. Effective political mobilization of community to achieve this goal may not be out of place. Having overcome the self-alienative psychology in the phase of the 'partition syndrome', Muslims in India have now already acquired a new cultural identity. It is now imperative for them to evolve a paradigm of Urdu education which harmonizes with their cultural aspirations on the one hand, and on the other, empowers them to be partners in social, political, and economic modernization of the Indian society.

Apart from the promotive role, the Muslim elite and middle classes should also set credible example by their own espousal of the cause of Urdu education through active participation and patronage. There seems to be a notable difference between the lower or lower-middle class Muslims and their upper and middle class compeers in respect of support to Urdu education. The lower and lower-middle class Muslims send their children to Urdu medium schools or Madarsa schools because for them better options of schooling are not available. This is not so for the upper and middle class Muslims. It is a paradox that better jobs and avenues for social and economic mobility are not available without access to modern education from which the present Urdu education remains alienated. This problem deserves further empirical investigation. The perception of the Muslim masses, however, about the double standards practised by the elite who patronize English medium private or convent schools while professing oral commitment to education through Urdu medium, is part of a general pattern relevant to all other regional languages including Hindi. Market forces, it seems, define this orientation. Urdu education, therefore, has to be modernized to overcome its market deficiencies.

There is a complex cultural basis for this discriminating phenomenon. It is related to the issues of what we have termed as 'symbolic domination' and 'legitimacy' of Urdu language in the linguistic community of India. The perceived prestige value of a language, its association with power structure, elite's cultural style and finally its market and economic significance matter a lot in this respect. These factors in totality go to shape the index of a language's symbolic domination or legitimacy. Paradoxically, if the ethnicization process in a cultural or religious community becomes exclusivist, then the value of symbolic domination of a language may get dissociated from market. Its economic significance is reduced and its impulses become totally culturological. There is some evidence to suggest that the Madarsa form of Urdu education of may face some such problems. There is need to address these issues in any systematic formulation of policies about the future pattern of Urdu education in our country.

It narrows down the job opportunities not only in the sectors of economy controlled by the state but also in the private sectors. During the past few decades we have witnessed some increase in job opportunities particularly in media and selected service sectors. However, its scope is seriously limited for graduates with degrees in the Urdu language or vernacular languages. Most youth, therefore, with such degrees, have either taken jobs in small-scale business enterprises, school teaching or other means of self-employment. Employment opportunities in high quality jobs in technical, professional and vocational services are not available to most Urdu graduates. Under these circumstances, there is urgent need for modernization of Urdu education as also for most other regional languages. It is essential to evolve a well-considered strategy for Urdu education and establish viable linkages with the demands of the Muslim community. The Muslim community will have itself to evolve a consensus on this issue because the institutional foci for available media of Urdu education are multiple and range from Madarsas to Urdu medium schools and colleges.

Learning from the past, it is anticipated that a consensus of this kind will take time to evolve as there are many complex factors at work. However, its pace can be accelerated as the economic and socio-political modernization increasingly encounters the challenges of globalization. In the meantime, innovative institutional and pedagogic alternatives for Urdu education which respond to the emergent demands of market and culture are urgently required. Voluntary efforts by institutions have a very crucial role to perform in this context. Modernization of the syllabi constitutes a very crucial and strategic aspect to establish viable linkages with the market, the state and the community's socio-cultural aspirations. For this, work needs to be undertaken both at the regional and all-India bases. The state-sponsored or state-supported institutional means available for promotion of Urdu literature and heritage (e.g., academics and institutes) and have a corpus of talent should be involved in such exercises. It may also be necessary to coordinate modernization of syllabi in consultation with relevant institutions such as the departments of education in the states and at the Centre and also the organized industries and corporations. The latter are likely to offer greater opportunities of future employment.

This problem cannot be examined in purely culturological terms. The pressures of job opportunities, economy and market govern educational choices in contemporary societies. The negative impact of market on educational-linguistic choices is sharper and more painful in societies with lower levels of social and economic development. In economically advanced societies, its displacement effects are absorbed by the policy of social welfare and flexibility of choices in education and job opportunities. Such flexibility is very limited or not available at all in developing societies.

In conclusion, it may be stated that a paradigm for the promotion of Urdu education should have sensitivity for social, cultural, economic and political aspirations of the Muslim community in India. The community response would have to be integrated with the institutional processes that influence processes of legitimation and identity formation. These processes, however, do not operate in isolation. The factors which deeply influence them arise from the actual and expected responses form the state, the market, and the elite and middle classes within the Muslim community. It also depends upon the manner in which Muslim community strategically locates itself about its perception of its cultural and religious identity.

References

Bourdieu, P., *Language and Symbolic Power*, Cambridge: Polity Press 1991.

Farouqui, A., "Emerging Dilemma of the Urdu Press in India: A Viewpoint", *South Asia, New Series*, Vol. XVIII, No.2, December 1995.

---, "Future Prospect of Urdu in India", *Mainstream*, Annual Number, 1992.

---, *Economic & Political Weekly*, Vol. XXIX No. 14, April 1994.

Manzoor Alam, M., "Indian Muslims: Challenges of 21st Century", *Academy Journal*, May 1-31, 1998.

Singh, Khushwant, "With Malice Towards One and All", *The Hindustan Times*, April 25, 1998.

Singh, K.S., *People of India: An Introduction*, Calcutta: Anthropological Survey of India, 1992.

7

The Desired Role of Political Leadership in Economic Reforms

In a broad sense, political leadership is oriented to the acquisition of power in order to utilize it for the collective mobilization of people to achieve the desired goals. Leadership is, therefore, purposive as well as normative in orientation. The definition of the 'desirable' or the normative aspect of leadership is located in history, social structure and cultural background of the society and its external surroundings. This somewhat structuralist notion of political leadership has its exceptions since we also come across instances where 'individual' leaders emerged with gifted charismatic entrepreneurial qualities. They usher in momentous changes in society. Sometimes such changes may have implications for the global political and economic order (Young, 1991; Ionescu, 1991; Ikenberry, 1996). The tendency, therefore, to analyze the nature and direction of social and economic policies of nations as articulated by political leadership in mere structuralist terms, such as the product of 'the world capitalist system' (Wallerstein, 1979) or 'global economic and technological hegemonism' etc. (Rapkin, 1990) have their limitations despite having many other explanatory advantages. In our own country, the phenomenon of leadership of

Gandhi or Nehru cannot be explained by using the method of structural determinism.

Yet, the contemporary changes in the role of political leadership and the degree of congruence that it shows with the desired values and the normative expectations of society are deeply influenced by the social, cultural and techno-economic changes taking place in the society and the world at large. Similarly, these forces of change also create situations of disenchantment from the political leadership. There are visible signs of such disenchantment within our own country and also at the global level today. These processes have meaningful implications for understanding the desired role of political leadership in the process of contemporary economic reforms. It appears that the industrial, technological and economic changes which today have a global dimension, have also led to the disintegration of the traditional values, institutions and the cultural identities. In the Euro-American context it may be witnessed in the feeling of alienation that members of society have in relation to the basic institutions such as family and community. It is also reflected in the breakdown of the Enlightenment ideology and the rise of post-modernism (Fukuyama, 1992; Touraine, 1995). These cultural and ideological tensions have seriously affected the polity and perception of the leadership role. It can be witnessed both in the developed and the developing countries. The historicity of the two situations is, however, different. In the developing nations such as India the problem is more complex where the tensions of economic underdevelopment combine with those of aspirations for cultural modernization.

LEADERSHIP CRISIS: GLOBAL AND NATIONAL DIMENSIONS

At the global level, there is toady a rethinking about some of the basic political values, institutions and their functions. The notions of citizenship, democracy (particularly, processes of representation, accountability, participation and openness etc.) and civil society are being critically reviewed. There exists a degree of disenchantment form the citizenship role and its increasing inefficacy even in the rich western democracies. It has led to an acute awareness first, of the need for 'reinventing democracy' (Hirst and Khilnani, 1996) by bringing about radical structural and institutional reforms in the polity, and secondly, there is increasing affirmation of the need to position the civil society in contradistinction with the state in a conscious manner. It is felt that between the two megaliths----the bureaucratic state on the one hand, and the heartless industrial corporations or the markets on the other, the citizen invariably suffers. About the citizenship role in the United State's democracy it is opined:

> "They (citizens) are passively serviced (or passively exploited) by the massive, busy-body, bureaucratic state where the world 'citizen' has no resonance and the only relevant civic act is voting (which less than half the eligible electorate engages in); or they sign on to the selfishness and the radical individualism of the private sector, where the word 'citizen' has no resonance and the only relevant activity is consuming (which just about every body engages in). Be a 'citizen', and vote the public scoundrels out of public office and/or be a consumer and exercise your private rights on behalf of your private interests; those are the only remaining obligations of much diminished office of American citizen" (Barber, 1996:151).

Similarly, crisis in a democracy is reflected in the decline of the political parties, abridgement of the role of the nation-state in the public governance due mainly to the increasing complexity and diversity in public services. There is increasing preference for managerial and professional dependency among political leaders replacing the "articulate language of political ideas". It has led to the reduction of democracy to a state where "it has become little more than a plebiscite; thus elections empower and legitimate rulers who govern in essentially undemocratic (top-down) ways" (Hirst, 1996: 107). Ascendancy of the market and the process of globalization have in the West weakened the mass political parties. Parties become oligopolies seeking to control and manipulate the behaviour of voters. The terms of their competition are increasingly set by modern media, whose general influence has been "towards trivialization and personalization of politics, as well as setting the agenda of debate by defining what counts as sound policy. The ignorance of the electorate about most public policy matters is reinforced by media and little countervailing pressure is now exerted either by civic education in schools or by alternative education programmes in the community" (Gamble, 1996:127).

This fear about the "hollowing out of democracy", both in the USA and the UK, has contributed to the search for new institutional innovations, new modalities of relationship between the market and democracy and has contributed to the added impetus for strengthening civil society through such civic institutions as the public interest groups, foundations, voluntary associations, civic groups (councils of users for all public services and of workers in work places etc.), schools, neighbourhoods and local communities. These, and such other institutions of the civil society are envisaged to perform a mediating function between the near monopolistic expanse of the power of the markets and corporations on the one hand, and on the other, of the over-corporatization and diminishing accountability of the state due to the expanded role of what Robert Dahl (1985) calls 'guardianship enclave' of the specialist in the process of governance. Hence, the emphasis upon the plural, associative and micro-democratic processes and institutions in society.

The need for these institutional reforms in polity coincides with the perception of a global crisis in leadership. "If there is one consistent complaint in politics around the world today, it is about the absence of leadership—local, national, global... The problem is everywhere. From the White House through Congress and down into the streets, there runs a cacophony of voices in which no single voice seems to sustain and rise from the crowd. Moreover, this is not just a problem in the United States. From London to Hamburg, Moscow to Tokyo, leadership seems to be in short supply" (Colonius, 1995 in Ikenberry, 1996:387). Diagnosis of this crisis has indeed to be undertaken keeping in view first, the global social and economic changes ushered in by the technologies of communication, new trade and market networks and the global emergence of the consumerist cultures and sub-cultures, and secondly, it is also linked with the tensions of structural changes in the individual societies of the developed world. It arises out of the new processes of economic transformation in these societies, where the self-regulating and global systems of the market economy defines its own momentum quite out of control of the political institutions. It is based upon the post-industrial technologies of production of goods and services which contribute to growth without adequate employment generation. This, on the one hand, augments alienation of the individuals from the system and on the other, leads to unemployment and waste. The evidences in plenty suggest that these processes of change impact negatively upon the family values, community relationship and lifestyles. These also engender an ethical crisis in public conduct and in the interpersonal relationships since the one-sided ascendance of the utilitarian values creates voids in capitalism and its markets in terms of ethical values. Max Weber (1992) long predicted this outcome which converts capitalism into an 'iron cage'.

As we shift our focus from the developed to a developing nation such as India, the dimension of the leadership crisis assumes a more complex and multilayered form. Indeed, the crisis here is created because of the tensions generated by the inner-structural and cultural changes in the institutions of democracy, political parties, markets and the expansion of the global technologies of production and communication. But, our crisis also emanates from the shortcomings in the adaptation and institutionalization of many of these structures and institutions. The problem also surfaces due to the historically distinct processes of interface between social and cultural changes in India which includes unique character of our nation-building processes and the policies of economic reform.

LEADERSHIP AND ECONOMIC REFORM IN INDIA

The process of economic reforms in India has had its unique historicity. The national movement for independence did contribute to the formulation of a broad framework of an economic policy. Nevertheless, between Mahatma Gandhi and Jawaharlal Nehru, radical differences on many aspects of policy and approach persisted. Gandhi believed in the moral autonomy of the individual over the state. The state for him represented concentration of power in order to exercise organized form of violence. Nehru, in the beginning, had great faith in the role of the state as an agent to usher in radical economic and social changes. He let the Planning Commission exercise state control over the key industries and all other high points of the economy. By intellectual socialization, he was suspicious of markets and profit motives of the individual entrepreneurs and industrialists in respect of their commitment to public causes. He believed in the commanding role of the state to bring about the social and economic transformation. Evidences, however, suggest that with the passage of time, Nehru realized the limitations of stateism in economic policy and preferred a middle path between the state and private economic enterprises and between goals of democracy and socialism (Pai Panandikar, 1994). The credit for bringing about the basic economic reforms which constitute the foundation of our socio-economic structure today goes to Nehru. Some of these reforms include: abolition of feudalism and land reforms; creation of the vast extension network in agriculture; massive investment in agriculture-related science, technology, irrigation, fertilizer and petrochemicals; creation of solid infrastructure in scientific and industrial research and the investment in higher education etc. These reforms provided the basis for democratic, economic and social transformation in India. Nehru was not merely a political leader endowed with charisma, but also "as Prime Minister for seventeen years, he strove hard to coach Chief Ministers, MPs, MLAs and the general masses in the norm of democracy. The letters he wrote to the Chief Ministers almost every fortnight are in the most part lessons in democratic procedure" (Rajmohan Gandhi, quoted in Rudolph and Rudolph,1987:83-84). The impact of these steps and attempts towards political education of the public leaders as evident did not bear fruits. But the fruits of the economic and technological investment did result into the Green Revolution during the 1970s which triggered a major process of political and social change in rural India.

With the exception of agriculture, where the initiative partially rested with the peasant entrepreneurship, in other economic sectors such as banking, industry, trade, fiscal policies, labour laws, etc., the tight state control and monitoring was consciously pursued. Indira Gandhi nationalized the fourteen major banks in 1969 to enlarge the control of the state to generate resources for the public investment in priority areas. As the results suggest, the regime of controls, quotas and licenses did not succeed in giving dynamism to the economy. Both the economic and social situations worsened by mid-1970s, and the state of internal emergency had to be declared in 1975. However, during the post-emergency phase, Indira Gandhi realized the need for reforms; she even moved 'rightward' (Kohli, 1991). It may, however, be noted that about this time China under Deng Xioping moved away from Mao Tse Tung's economic policies of state control. The new micro-electronic revolution of 1970s had ushered in processes of globalization and information revolution. India began to increasingly realize how far it has been left behind its contemporary nations such as China had South Korea in matters of economic and social development (Pai Panandikar, 1994; Dereze and Sen, 1995). The external environment has also been changing, possibly adding impetus to the need for reforms. By 1980-81, following L.K. Jha Commission on Economic And Administrative Reforms, the policy of decontrol and automatic licensing for some key industries was initiated. The process, nevertheless, remained halting and could not get fully integrated with the national political agenda and vision.

Rajiv Gandhi was enthusiastic about the economic reforms. But these remained, however, constrained due to lack of party support. Particularly his attempt to do away with the policy of state-controlled import-substitution approach of the past was a major step towards liberalization. Little progress in this direction was achieved due to the alienation of grassroots leadership of the Congress from his techno-managerial method of political management. The Janata Dal regime that succeeded the Congress government headed by Rajiv Gandhi, got trapped into policies of financial and social populism, and the process of reforming the economy remained moribund. By 1991, a grave economic crisis engulfed the country as the foreign exchange reserve fell to just US $1.1 billion, sufficient only for two weeks' import. By June 1991, a new Congress government with P.V. Narsimha Rao as Prime Minister came to power. Dr. Manmohan Singh, the new Finance Minister, initiated the new policies of reform which set into notion the process of economic liberalization and global linkages of the economy.

In his budget speech, in July 1991, the Finance Minister indicated the gravity of the problem as also the need for alternative policy. He said: "The crisis in the economy is both acute and deep. We have not experienced anything similar in the history of independent India." He went on to sum up the issues: "The origins of the problem are directly traceable to large and persistent macro-economic imbalances and the low productivity of investment, in particular the poor rate of return on past investments. There has been an unsustainable increase in

Government expenditure. Budgetary subsidies with questionable social and economic impact have been allowed to grow to an alarming extent. The tax system still has many loopholes... The public sector has not been managed in a manner so as to generate large investible surpluses... The increasing difference between the income and expenditure of the government has led to a widening of the gap between the income and expenditure of the economy as a whole... This is reflected in the growing current account deficit in the balance of payments" (quoted in Pai Panandikar, 1994:37).

These reforms brought results. By 1994, the foreign exchange reserves which had fallen to $1.1 billion in 1991 rose to $13 billion. The exports grew substantially, and the imports were within manageable limits; the exchange rate of the rupee remained stable. Inflation which had reached 17 per cent in August 1991 came down below the double digit in 1994. The fiscal deficit came down to 5.7 per cent of the GDP in 1992-93 from 8.5 per cent in 1991 but rose again to 7.4 per cent in 1993-94 The inflation also reached a double digit figure in 1994 April, indicating lack of control on expenditure on account of populist pressures. Obviously, the pace of reforms had slowed down. The Congress lost the next election, and the coalition government of Prime Minister Devegowda worked out a minimum programme agenda in which economic reforms were sustained despite ideological difference among the coalition partners. Finance Minister Chidambram's budget of 1997 was hailed widely by the middle classes and the industrial leaders. It was remarkably bold in respect of tax reforms, further decontrolled the economy and aimed at bold monetary and fiscal reforms. It yielded better results as well: the foreign exchange reserves reached the level of $23 billions, the inflation declined to below 6 per cent, and the fiscal deficit came down at the level of about 5 per cent of the GDP.

The coalition government continued to operationalize and implements the agenda of economic reforms logically implicit in Dr. Manmohan Singh's policies of economic liberalization. However, in some sensitive areas such as the labour policy, disinvestment in the loss-making public sector industries and investment in some other areas of economy, etc., there was slow movement.

The political leadership has ultimately to provide not only the vision but also momentum to the economic reforms. In a liberal multi-party democracy of a federal nature such as India, with complex sets of the regional and sectional interest-groups, building consensus on the policy of economic reforms becomes essential. It requires both transparency and credibility in the decisions of the political leadership. It covers both the sequencing and direction of the economic reforms. The issue of 'desirability' of political leadership cannot be separated from the quality of commitment and credibility of the leaders. Moreover, consensus cannot be built or sustained without political leader's ability to present the agenda of economic reforms with a sense of empathy with the social, cultural and institutional limits and aspirations of the people. A consensual approach goes beyond the 'command politics' but remains sensitive to the genuine 'demands' of the major interest groups which together constitute the legitimate social and institutional fabric of the economy.

The new economic policies evoked mixed responses from different interest-groups in society. The business groups, viz., the Federation of Indian Chambers of Commerce and Industry (FICCI), the Associated Chambers of Commerce and Industries in India (ASSOCHAM) and the Confederation of Indian Industries (CII) etc., favoured the economic reforms. The Indian urban and professional middle classes generally approved of it. A small segment of the rural middle classes, that represent a section of the successful peasants and farmers (such as the Shetkari Sangathan and the Bhartiya Kisan Union etc.) have also offered support to the reforms demanding parity with industry and larger investment in agriculture. The opposition, however, comes from the organzied labour, concentrated largely in the public sector/ industries. A large segment of the rural peasantry is also suspicious that the new economic policies would expose them to unequal competition with the agro-multinationals leading ultimately to their dependency. India's about 40 per cent poor looked at these reforms with a feeling of anxious anticipation. Their continued poverty, illiteracy and unemployment made them vulnerable to suspicion, marginalized as they are in the political economy.

The consensus building on the issue of economic reforms, therefore, has to take into consideration these various interest-groups which pose formidable challenges to political leadership in a multi-party democracy. It calls for a strong credibility and commitment on the part of political leadership to strike an optimal or sustainable balance between imperatives of economic liberalization and globalization, on the one hand, and tailor them effectively to the programmes of social justice and welfare to protect the interests of the vulnerable sections of society, on the other. This 'middle path' of economic reforms may involve innovative yet difficult choices. The desired political leadership is the one which successfully accomplishes this task.

SOCIAL AND CULTURAL CONTEXTS

Such 'desired' leadership would have to set for itself credible ethical and normative standards, which invariably links the leadership role with the social and cultural processes of the society. The factors that social scientists have examined in this context are related to the social structure, cultural background and personality of the political leaders. Several studies have concluded that the processes of social mobility and structural changes in our society have affected the quality of political leadership over a period of time. The tensions of 'command' and 'demand' politics as discussed by Rudolphs (Rudolph and Rudolph, 1987) have led the political leadership in India to adopt manoeuvring and deviant tactics to enlarge their constituencies, based on short-term populist goals. This has sharpened the 'crisis of legitimacy' not only of the leadership but also that of the political institutions and the party system. This delegitimation extends to the relationship between the political leaders and bureaucrats as well. The leadership rôle is oriented more to the personality cult at the cost of erosion of the political institutions. In the poorer economies it also means that the level of control passes into the hands of "individuals rather than institutions" (Kohli, 1992:31). In the case of India, this situation is compounded with the exploitation of the sentiments of caste, religion, ethnicity and region. Often, in political calculations, these factors take a priority over the rational economic and political choices. Eventually, corruption and criminalization in politics and leadership roles begin which further erode the legitimacy and credibility of the political institutions and their ability to pursue economic reforms.

Compared to the western democracies, where a rethinking on the role of the state has triggered the demand for separation of the civil society from the party democratic apparatus, the situation in India is doubly fragile. Here, the foundations of both democracy and the civil society are weak, and in institutional terms, the civil society has yet to take its roots. The process of social change during the past fifty years has, no doubt, led to successes in some sectors of society. There are also sectors of major failures. The successes are reflected in the rise of a substantial, professional, entrepreneurial and educated middle class in the cities. It is followed by the growth of rural middle classes due largely to the Green Revolution. There is some evidence of social mobility also among the Dalits which is reflected in the growth of a middle class among the scheduled castes and scheduled tribes. This middle class, also termed as a "limited elite", is today articulate in cultural-political arena. The total number of the middle classes in India is estimated between 150 and 250 million which indicates the success of the past socio-economic policies. These changes, however, bring into wake major crises in the domains of political values, institutions and leadership. The social mobility has accelerated the feelings of caste and sectarianism which now increasingly define the scope of economic political processes. These often reflect adversely on the legitimacy of the institutions of the state, democracy and civil society.

The middle class values are also in transition. A sense of narrow self-serving utilitarianism pervades among them, irrespective of their origin (rural/urban) or occupation (profession/business/farming). They idealize values of democracy and personal ethic but paradoxically in their own behaviour it is seldom reflected (Singh, 1993). There exists, however, a consensus among all middle classes in support of economic policies ----of growth and social mobility. The virtues of higher levels of investment in industry, agriculture and infrastructure are recognized. The recent studies on peasant movements reveal that instead of opposing the policies of economic reform insistence of the farmers is for a larger share of investment in agriculture, and they demand parity in fiscal and trade policies comparable to the industrial sector (Gupta, 1988; Steffan, 1992). This suggests that despite strident invocation of the primordialities of caste, religion and ethnicity as resources for political mobilization, the Indian political leadership does have an expanding space available where the legitimate norms of 'associative democracy' and civil society are supported. This space, which is bound to expand in the future years, provides strength to the cosmopolitan policies of social and economic reforms.

IMPEDIMENTS IN THE GROWTH OF DESIRED FORM OF LEADERSHIP

The crisis in the growth of the desired form of political leadership, though a global phenomenon, has a deeper root in India. A degenerative erosion of the party system in almost all political parties has taken place. Institutional politics has been increasingly replaced by personalized politics, and political commitment is increasingly defined as commitment not to political principles or values but to personal loyalties. Social structural impediments such as high degree of illiteracy (adult literacy rate of all ages combined and seven years and above being 52 per cent by 1991 census) (Dreze and Sen, 1996: 213), and poverty of about 40 per cent of the population reinforce these tendencies. Apart from generating contradictory pulls in the social and economic policies, this also creates structural and cultural cleavages in the evolution of the civil institutions and their effective functioning. The articulation of rights qua a 'citizen' takes a back seat, and the mobilization of primordial ties takes precedence in a mode of patron-client relationships. It not only weakens the standards of accountability of political leadership but also explains their loss of credibility in society.

Consequently, the level of corruption in the political, bureaucratic, professional and business sectors of society has mounted to an alarming extent. The personalized mode of the exercise of political power has increased the nexus between politicians-bureaucrats and criminals. How far this nexus bedevils our polity and democratic system has been examined by the N.N. Vohra Committee. A large number of politicians and bureaucrats now tend to offer protection to criminal elements, work in league with them and also support them in cases of criminal prosecution. Few political parties are exception to this phenomenon, and among most of them there is a competition to safeguard their own criminal elements. Madhava Godbole (1997), the former Union Home Secretary has termed this as: "My thug is better than your thug" syndrome among the political parties.

The social scientists have been studying the phenomenon of corruption from the sociological, economic and political perspectives (Jain, 1979). Some of them have sought to explain it from the perspective of cultural relativism. But it seems that corruption in India has increased due mainly to the failure of institutions, over-centralization of discretionary powers and absence of transparency and accountability in pubic decision-making. The state has over-extended itself and left enormous discretionary powers with the political leaders and bureaucrats to distribute quota, licenses, permits, etc., which in an environment of monopolistic scarcity has led to corruption. Innovative institutional and civil safeguards have been non-existent or wherever they exist are ineffective. The institutional breakdown explains to a large extent the pathology of corruption in our society.

LIMITS OF POLITICAL LEADERSHIP IN ECONOMIC REFORMS

The political leadership has, to play a leading role in the economic reforms. But there are factors which delimit their role in this task. These limits arise out of processes intrinsic to contemporary economic globalization and also within each country due to the mobilization of interest-groups. The structure of economic and social inequalities within each state sharpens the resistance to economic reforms. The uplinking of the national economies with the global forces such as, trade, banking and tariff policies etc., compromise the autonomy of governments to peruse the reform policies in an adaptive manner. It also tells upon their social welfare policies (Michaels, 1997; Barber, 1996). It is recognized that the market forces abridge the autonomy of the political leadership's role not only within the country concerned, but also (in a strategic sense) internationally. For instance, the "strategic use of domestic market openings" brought the USA and UK to the status of the hegemonic powers (Ikenberry, 1996; Strange, 1988). The significance of both the management of economic reforms as well as the aspirations and needs of the interest-groups has to be recognized in India in order to augment the pace of social and economic reforms.

In a relatively less established fashion, the limit to the desired role of leadership in India has been associated with the culture and the personality structure of its people (Kakar, 1978; Desai, 1995). Psychologists and social anthropologists have studied the child-rearing processes, the roles of mother and father in child socialization and formation of child's identities, etc., and have concluded that to a significant degree the disjunction between personal ambition and public morality among people in India including the political leadership arises out of malformation of the "ontogeny of the Indian self-esteem" which is nurtured due to anxieties of childhood socialization peculiar to India (Desai, 1995:259). These views have, however, been long since contested by sociologists and social anthropologists (Pocock, 1961) on account of 'reductionism'. Indeed, viewed from the angle of personality formation, the desired leadership role which Desai outlines as "leaders who work selflessly, which often includes not seeking power, with an inexhaustible supply of self-worth and an untiring capacity of being in tune with their admirers" (Desai, 1995:264), is a cultural and not a mental or psychic reality. The roles of the cultural and moral factors are widely recognized in the formation of desired political leadership. But, the ideal cultural prerequisite for this evades almost all societies in the world. And, each society must address this problem in the context of its own historicity. No doubt, the moral commitment of the political leadership is necessary for the credibility of political sponsorship of reforms (Haslett, 1997) under capitalist economic order.

AUGMENTING THE DESERTED ROLE OF POLITICAL LEADERSHIP

Implicitly, our examination of the social and political processes above also suggests the ways and means for augmenting the desired role of political leadership in economic reforms. It obviously begins with working out a national consensus on the policy and pace of economic reforms, and then setting into motion the institutional and financial mechanism for their effective implementation. The changes in the structural and social background of political leadership during the past fifty years has considerably eroded the influence of the 'hegemonic classes' and in order to carry credibility economic reforms will have to be orchestrated with sensitivity to the emergent social forces and interest groups. The changing composition of leadership is evident from the changing social background of MLAs and MPs in the Legislative Assemblies and the Parliament respectively, over the years. This has introduced a culture of 'subalternity', 'protest', and demands in the political culture of our society.

The first requisite, therefore, of a desired role of the political leadership in economic reforms is their ability to mediate among diverse structural and cultural demands in a manner that optimizes consensus and minimizes conflicts. A strategic use of the policies of economic reforms with welfare measures can help realize this consensus. The interests of the peasants, workers and petty artisans will have to be protected by viable integration of the rural economy with the industrial economy. Also, it may be necessary to ensure that the state continues its role in effective implementation of the welfare policies, such as , universalization of education and investment in public health. A strategic balance and functional linkage between various sectors of economy are prerequisites for the political leadership to manage structural imbalances that are bound to emerge in the processes of economic reforms. (Bangura, 1992; Singh, 1993). The implementation of the policies of distributive justice, such as the reservation policy, empowerment of the weaker sections, reduction in gender inequalities and decentralization of power through empowerment of the local bodies, like PRIs, form essential steps towards accelerating the degree of consensus about economic reforms. Contrary to this, some evidence suggests that in the pursuit of policies of 'state minimalism' for reduction of fiscal deficits, governments and political leadership have already eroded funds vital for welfare activities meant for the poor. Instead of reducing unproductive and wasteful expenses (Human Development Report, 1997) the expedient by leaders breeds disenchantment from economic reforms.

INSTITUTIONAL CHANGES

To perform an innovative role in a democracy the political leadership requires meaningful institutional support to maintain its credibility and accountability. The new expectations from political leadership in the process of the globalization of economy and the communication and information systems, together with corporatization of the economic and the political institutions, have led to rethinking on these issues even in the advanced economies of the democratic West. The situation in India, however, calls for greater efforts as here we encounter apathy among the political leadership to the institutional norms already existing in the books. This goes along with the urgent need for further institutional reforms. There is need to streamline, cleanse and render the decision-making process of the leadership more credible and transparent. We face difficulties because unlike in the West, in our case, the institutional foundation of democracy remains weak and the civil society is yet to be born.

To attain desired norms in the political behaviour and for the leadership to accelerate the pace of economic reforms, it is imperative first, that the existing institutional structures of the polity are made more responsive. Wherever institutions have become outmoded suitable reforms or replacements be introduced. Moreover, additional institutional innovations in the polity may be required. Among the existing institutional structure requiring further reforms we may include the electoral reforms in consultation with the political parties, effective implementation of the devolution of power to the states where agreement already exists and continual review of the need for further devolution and decentralization of decision-making to the states for implementation of the policies of economic reforms, and empowerment of the institutions of Lokpal and

Lokayukt in a credible form to monitor and take action in cases of the violation of the instituted norms and standards by political leadership. Mechanism may be evolved to enforce strict adherence by political parties to the party constitution in matters of electoral representation, appointment of office bearers and commitment to declared policies of political action. Parties may also have to evolve commonly agreed norms for nomination of persons of character to seek elections for political offices. There should be mechanism for enforcement and accountability in the cases of violation of evolved norms. Institutional mechanism would have to be evolved in this respect both by the Election Commission and the political parties. There is widespread worry in India among the public and the political leadership about the increasing criminalization in politics and about the nexus between the criminal mafia, the political leadership and the bureaucracy. Suitable institutional support to curb and eliminate this is urgently required. It may require streamlining of the structure and functioning of the reinforcement agencies of the state and transparency in economic decision-making.

One major area of institution-building necessary for desired role of political leadership is that of consolidating the foundation of the civil society. The voter in our country has yet to achieve the status of the citizen. Poverty, illiteracy, cultural and social oppression, due to reasons of caste, gender, religion and ethnicity etc., have worked as traditional impediments to its evolution. The civil consciousness is relatively weaker also among the educated and economically better-off middle classes now comprising over two hundred million in numbers. The role of the non-governmental organizations remains largely confined to the areas of social and economic development. Civil rights movements have yet to gather roots in the mainstream life of our society. The strengthening of the civil society has close linkages with the evolution of what is called 'associative democracy'. It requires mobilization of people into interest-groups which leads to the formation of associations based not on primordiality but occupations, professional skills and other cosmopolitan interests (Singh, 1993). These associative organizations may supplement and reinforce the organs of the civil society such as the human rights organizations, citizens' councils, citizens' jury and 'deliberative forums' (Hirst, 1996; Barber, 1996).

The changes in the technology of communication and information and the increasing diversification and corporatization of economy have changed the classical notion of 'liberalism' based on individual rights. These are seen today in a new light specially in respect of the relationship between state and civil society. "In a period when statist and socialist solutions have become ineffective and politically unviable, we are left with a rhetoric of individual rights in politics and the advocacy of market principles in society...To recognize this is not just an issue of the economics of competition, it is also a problem for governance. The hegemony of liberalism means that most attempts to counter or ameliorate weak economic regulations and social accountability are half-hearted or ineffective" (Hirst, 1996:101). The Indian experience fully illustrates this situation, and hence the need to strengthen both the associative organizations and the organs of civil society in India.

For instance, the Indian state policy regarding the citizens' right to information is one of the weakest links between the norms of political accountability and the role of the civil society. Only now some systematic rethinking and action on this aspect of our political and civil life has been initiated. Despite several Administrative Reforms Committees, action on the information-related rights of the citizens could not be initiated mainly due to the apathy of the politicians and bureaucrats. Most antiquated colonial rules and regulations have been allowed to persist in an overarching culture of statism and regulated economy without countenancing norms of responsibility and accountability. Not only such rules and regulation should be reviewed but action should also be initiated to empower citizens with a 'right to information' in areas of governmental decision-making to encourage transparency, accountability and responsiveness in the implementation of public policies. This would arrest the rise in corrupt and authoritarian practices of the political leadership and administrative functionaries at various levels. This would also help in the creation of people-friendly and investment-friendly environment commensurate with new economic reform policies.

THE ETHICAL AND CULTURAL VALUES

The enduring aspect of a desired political leadership depends upon its credibility with the people. The traditional values and ethical precepts play an important role in this process. The traditional Bhakti movement, with its deep roots among the Indian peasantry, had ethicized their outlook and lifestyle that lasted for centuries. It cherished a form of rationalism with disdain towards the Brahmin orthodoxy---religious and cultural. The middle classes in India have been known to profess values of spiritual asceticism with pragmatic commitment to action projects. In totality, Indian culture and ethical values did not wholly anchor themselves in 'other-wordly asceticism' as western thinkers such as Max Weber and Gunnar Myrdal concluded. The values cherished by Indians, whether they were professional middle classes, aristocracy, traders, peasants or workers, had a dualistic feature: spiritual or other-worldliness in transcendental values and pragmatism in respect of wordly or material values. This explains the 'enigma' of the rise of the entrepreneurial classes, communities of professionals and managers in the cities as well as the Green Revolution by the rich peasantry in the countryside. The material anchorage of values and lifestyles of the people of India is affirmed by a recent study of 4,634 communities (in the whole of India). It concludes: "We are largely a smoking, drinking and meat-eating people" (Singh, 1992:65).

The understanding of this aspect of culture and ethical values of the Indian people is necessary. It explains, on the one hand, the tensions and contradictions in the commitment to new democratic values and on the other, its continued resilience. Despite contradictions in the role of the political leadership seen in the context of expected institutional norms, this probably explains why we have witnessed a general consensus among political parties and leadership in India on the policies of economic reform. The pragmatic aspect of the traditional cultural values of the Indian people resonates through such manifestations. It also explains the supremely adaptive and flexible response of the people towards institutions and values required for industrial, technological and economic modernization.

But pragmatism bereft of ethical content poses threat to the systems---be they political, economic or cultural. A large part of hiatus that we witness today in the role of the political leadership as between their selfish pragmatism and their credible or responsible performance in accordance with the democratic norms, can possibly be explained by this cultural dualism in our society. The nature of social mobility and crisis of aspiration of classes in varied strata of society have further made the process difficult. It is, therefore, necessary to operationalize mechanisms for conformity to the desired political values and norms among the political leaders. This would require institutional innovations. For example, the constitution of 'ethics committees' to monitor and enforce the expected norms by the political parties, political caucuses, assemblies and parliament on a voluntary and self-governing basis can be a very effective institutional innovation to achieve the goals of value-oriented politics. In addition, continual programmes of educational camps, tours and travels may be organized for the elected representatives and the political leadership (MLAs, MPs and those holding ministerial positions in government or holding offices in the political parties). Exposure to the emergent comparative political institutions and innovations in other democracies may also constitute a part of such educational and training programmes.

All over the world, politics is increasingly being corporatized. The use of telecommunication and computer technology, use of management methods for running the party and political programmes, increasing role of the professionals and specialists in political decision-making are such steps that will accentuate the desired role of the political leadership in economic reforms. There are techno-managerial transformations in society that cannot be long avoided. Despite the dilemmas that such changes pose to the norms of representative democracy (Miller, 1996; Margetts and Hirst, 1996), these technological innovations are going to stay and grow in volume in the years to come. These may require, therefore, continuous renewal of skills and exposure of the political leadership to the new values of management and ethicization of politics. The needs is to work out methods of operationalization to reinforce ethical standards in political behaviour at various levels of political leadership.

References

Bangure, Yusuf, "Authoritarian Rule and Democracy in Africa: A Theoretical Discourse", in Lars Rudeback, in *When Democracy Makes Sense* (ed.), Uppasala: Uppasala University Press, 1922

Barber, B.R., "Three Challenges to Reinventing Democracy", in Paul Hirst and Sunil Khilnani (eds.), *Reinventing Democracy*, Cambridge: Blackwell Publishers, 1996.

Colonius, Erik, "Take Me To Your Leader", *Hemispheres*, April 1995, quoted in "The Future of International Leadership", *Political Science Quarterly*, Vol.III, No.3, 1996.

Dahl, R., *Controlling Nuclear Weapons*, Syracuse: Syracuse University Press, 1985.

Dreze, Jean and Amartya Sen, *India: Economic Development and Social Opportunity*, Delhi: Oxford University Press, 1996.

Desai, P.N., "Personality Politics: A Psychoanalytic Perspective", in Upendra Baxi and Bhiku Parekh (eds.), *Crisis and Change in Contemporary India*, New Delhi: Sage Publications, 1995.

Fukuyama, F., *The End of History and the Last Man*, London: Hamish Hamilton, 1992.

Gamble, Andrew, "The Limits of Democracy", in Hirst and Khilnani (eds.), *Reinventing Democracy*, Cambridge, Blackwell, 1996.

Godbole, M., "Crime and Blandishment:My Thug is Better than Your Thug", *The Times of India*, April 18, 1997.

Gupta, Dipankar "Country-Town Nexus and Agrarian Mobilization: Bhartiya Kisan Union as an Instance", *Economic and Political Weekly*, Vol.23, No.51, 1988.

Haslett, D.W., *Capitalism with Morality*, London: Oxford University Press, 1997.

Hirst, P. and S. Khilnani (eds.), *Reinventing Democracy*, Cambridge: Blackwell, 1996.

Hirst, P.Q., "Democracy and Civil Society" in Hirst and Khilnani, *op.cit.*

Ikenberry, G.J., "The Future of International Leadership", *Political Science Quarterly*, Vol. III, No. 3, 1996.

Ionescu, G., *Leadership in an Independent World: The Statesmanship of Adenauer, De Gaulle, Thacher, Reagan and Gorbachev,* Westview, 1991.

Jain, R.K., "Sociology of Corruption in the Developing Societies: Morality in Theory and Practice", *Philosophy and Social Action*, Vol. 3-4, 1979.

Kakar, Sudhir, *The Inner World: Childhood and Society in India*, Delhi: Oxford University Press, 1978.

Kohli, Atul, *Democracy and Discontentment: India's Growing Crisis of Governability*, New York, Cambridge University Press, 1991.

Michaels, James, "In Conversation" (with Jagdeep Worah), *Sunday Observer*, May 11-17, 1997.

Pai Panandikar, V.A., " The Present Indian Economic Situation", *Indian Horizon*, Vol. 43, No. 3, 1994.

Pocock, D., "Psychological Approaches and the Judgement of Reality" in L. Dumont and D. Pocock (eds.), *Contribution to Indian*

Sociology, Paris: Mouton and Co., 1961.

Rapkin, David, F.P., *World Leadership and Hegemony*, Boulder Co: Lynne Rienner Publications, 1990.

Rudolph L. and Rudolph S., *In Persuit of Lakshmi*, 1987, Bombay: Orient Longman Ltd.

Singh, S.K., *People of India: An Introduction*, Calcutta: Anthropological Survey of India, 1992.

Singh, Yogendra, *Social Change in India: Crisis and Resilience*, Delhi: Har Anand Publishers, 1993.

Steffan, Lindberg, "Peasants for Democracy? Farmers Agitation and the State in India", in Lars Rudebeck(ed.), *When Democracy Makes sense*, Uppasala: Uppasala University, 1992.

Strange, Susan, *States and Markets*, London: Pinter Publishers, 1988.

Touraine, Alain, *Critique of Modernity*, Cambridge: Blackwell Publishers, 1995.

UNDP, *Human Development Report*, 1997.

Wallerstein, Immanuel, *The Capitalist World Economy*, New York: Cambridge University Press, 1979.

Weber, Max, *Protestant Ethnic and the Spirit of Capitalism*, London: Routledge, 1992.

Young, Oran, "Political Leadership and Regime Formation: On the Development of Institutions in International Society", *International Organization*, No. 45, 1991.

8

A Life-World of Disenchantment

Modernity, Ethnicity and Pluralism

It is a matter of immense pleasure and great privilege for me to dedicate this lecture to the sacred memory of late Prof. S.C. Dube. My association with him goes back to 1958, when I had just started my career as a lecturer of sociology at the Institute of Social Sciences, Agra. Prof. Dube had by then published his celebrated book on the Indian village, which had drawn the attention of sociologists and social anthropologists, nationally and internationally. To my mind, it was the first attempt by an Indian sociologist to bring the scientific method of social anthropology to bear upon the study of social structure of an Indian village. He ventilated through this study the basic underlying factors which shape the making of Indian society and culture. It was no doubt a microscopic study. But it also had immense implications for understanding the larger Indian society and culture. This contribution led Prof. Dube to his other successive books and papers through which he analyzed the processes of social change in India. The planned method of social transformation of the Indian society and economy was ushered in by our national

---

This paper is a lecture delivered by the author at the Jammu University, J&K in memory of late Prof. S.C. Dube.

leadership about the mid-1950s onwards, and the rural society occupied a pivotal place in the chain of several institutional reforms. Prof. Dube, through his studies of community development programmes in the country, considerably influenced the policies and administration of this programme. He also occupied some of the highest offices of policy-making and administration in the field of rural community planning in India.

Through various internationally acclaimed academic works, giving leadership to several prestigious academic institutions (including the vice-chancellorship of this esteemed university) and having been deservedly decorated with several academic honours and awards, Prof. Dube had reached the peak of his academic worldview where he realized the significance of civilization and its crisis, in a deeper and broader perspective to understand the processes of social change and planning in India. This led him to devote systematic attention to the analysis of modernization and its linkages with ideology, social structure and power. This also was probably instrumental in his most perceptive critique of Indian culture and society originally written in Hindi. He strongly felt that in order to come to meaningful grip with the aspiration for freedom, and economic, social and cultural enlightenment, it was necessary first to come to terms with one's native language. Language being the source of legitimation and symbolic power.

II

This memorial lecture on "A Life-World of Disenchantment: Modernity, Ethnicity and Pluralism" is addressed to Prof. Dube's quintessential intellectual involvement with this theme, which in substance constitutes the enigma of human condition not only in contemporary India but all over the world. A life-world for a society is constituted by a set of elements drawn from history and existential determinants of human situation. Just as for an individual his biography sums up the chronology of his body and consciousness, the notion of life-world philosophically represents changing configurations of the vital- existential and historical processes of society which shape its well-being. No doubt, a life-world by its very constitution is grounded in ideology. It is from this source that the notion of societal well-being is legitimated. The existential determinants of society, such as population, access to means of livelihood, social stratification and distribution of power and wealth, etc., are ever in the process of transition triggered by forces internal and external to society. The temporal pattern of occurrence of these forces or encounter with them constitutes societal history.

Disenchantment is a philosophical expression and also an ideological phenomenon. It links history with mythology. Indeed, demythologization which follows the supremacy of the scientific worldview and which inaugurated the notion of modernity is intimately connected with the process of disenchantment. Max Weber, who among the classical sociologists made disenchantment the central theme of his theory of rationalization, primarily based his analysis on a shift from the traditional-prophetic worldview of societies to modern societies based on scientific reason. The traditional society sanctified the revealed tradition, principle of sacred hierarchy and transcendental sources of legitimation of values and cultural practices in society. In a modern society, not prophecy but reason, not hierarchy but equality, not vocation or calling but work, not sacred meanings but pragmatic instrumentalities and rational legal rules govern day to day life of the people. The laws of the universe, even though probabilistic, are understandable to a modern mind as they constitute a system of mathematical precision. This applies to systems that are not only orderly but even those which are catastrophic or chaotic in character. It is these normative shifts in the rationalization of the life-world and its cosmology which defined the notion of modernity.

Disenchantment is inherent in the historic break from traditional worldview on life and nature which science inaugurated especially by introducing a perspective on the world as comprising "a totality of empirical things and a complex of empirical attributes". As Ernest Cassierer (1966:1) writes: "Wherever philosophy sought to establish a theoretical view of the world, it was confronted not so much by immediate phenomenal reality as by the mythical transformation of this reality... Long before the world appeared to consciousness as a totality of empirical things and a complex of empirical attributes it was manifested as an aggregate of mythical powers and effects." This mythic mode of thinking and institutionalization of societies which the paradigm of modernity has supposedly replaced came about as a result of two factors: first, the revolution within the sacred worldview of societies, and secondly, by a renaissance in science and technology which triggered the industrial revolution. Both developments contributed to the growth of capitalism and its consequent cultural and institutional innovations. The internal revolution within the sacred worldview is vividly described by Max Weber in his *Protestant Ethic and the Spirit of Capitalism.* The changing notions of predestination and transcendental nature of God which protestantism of Calvin ushered in, shifted the moral responsibility from the sacred brotherhood to the individual believer. It made individual alone accountable for his time-budgeting, called upon him to work hard, lead a life of puritan simplicity and employ all his entrepreneurial skills "to make this world kingdom of God on earth". It also made him lonely and anxious because mere conformity to such ethical conduct indeed did not ensure 'grace' of God. Grace required 'His' inscrutable pleasure. This uncertainty about bestowal of grace among the faithful led to competitive search for excellence, hard work, rational accounting and culturally reinforced the rise of capitalism. The revolution in science only reinforced this cultural revolution towards rational capitalism in the western society.

Disenchantment, however, soon followed. According to Weber, the institution of capitalism which enjoyed the backing of men and women in sacred robe soon became an 'iron cage' when sensuality replaced puritanism, and utilitarian instrumentalities supplanted the ethics of transcendent meanings and values. Philosophers have successfully explained this irony by saying "that modern man is disenchanted in so far as he knows the world does not have an 'objective' meaning 'and that it falls to man' primarily to create objective meaning, and the interconnection of meaning, the relation to reality, in so far as *his* relation is to *create* meaning theoretically and practically" (Vattimo, 1992: 93).

LOGIC OF DISENCHANTMENT: CRISIS IN THEORY

As we encounter the contemporary situation, the logic of disenchantment inherent in the notion of modernity, has unfolded social, cultural and existential forces that lead up to collapse of theory. The paradigm of scientific explanation of social realities, a contribution of the Enlightenment ideology, has long come under clouds. Limits of empiricism have been exemplified with the growth of ethno-science and ethno-methodology; teleological assumptions implicit in most treatises on social order and change, which lean heavily upon the functional theory, have been discredited both by those who profess an open-ended nomological (mathematical) approach to the study of society and thus seemingly extend the reach of the disenchantment ideology, as also by those who prefer to undertake an interpretive or phenomenological analysis of social reality giving primacy to configurations of meanings and symbolic forms implicit in social relationships. The new methods of textual or discourse analysis have extended the reach of such analysis by highlighting the significance of hidden agenda implicit in most interpretive paradigms of theory. It is felt that the impulse to gain domination or power is inherent in most texts. They do not illuminate but distract by subterfuges, strategies of displacement of meanings and often undertake rationalization of the irrational. Foucault's thesis on the "archaeology of knowledge" and Lacan's new-Freudian perspective on the "nature of language" mutually celebrate the role of the irrational in everyday life of common man. Add to this is Derrida's thesis of "deconstruction". According to Derrida, the text does not reveal the underlying or unstated stratagems of the writer, and writing artfully projects a notions of system, rationality or consensus which indeed, are mere contrivances. All this adds up to debunking of theory in social sciences.

The intellectual nihilism, implicit in these post-modern views on social science theory, is merely a manifestation of double disenchantment: first, it is marked by alienation from tradition which the worldview of modernity inaugurated, and secondly, it is symptomatic of the varied aberrations of ideology and culture in the contemporary post-capitalist society. Optimists had anticipated that the decadence of values and meanings following the utilitarian model of capitalism which encased the soul of the contemporary humans in the 'iron cage' could be salvaged by material progress and selective institutional reforms. That, at least the 'iron cage' could be converted through a softer and revitalized life-world into a 'rubber cage'. It does not seem to happen. Ernest Gellner (1987;1992) as an optimist, says: "The success of disenchantment in manipulating the natural and social worlds may free up the time to pursue other activities, leisure and education among them." Yet, he is unable to pronounce with finality as to the nature of the relationship that may exist between the industrialism of the 'iron cage' and the succorance of the 'rubber cage' providing leisure time, education and consumerist indulgences. Gellner is right in his rejection of the post-modern ideology but he still shows acute ambiguity in his attempt to salvage the problem of contemporary industrial society from its drift towards meaninglessness and self-alienation. We will come to term with these issues more objectively when we relate the issue of disenchantment with clearly observable aspect of our everyday life-world.

Yet, before we deal with this aspect of the problem, it is natural to ask: how does the process of disenchantment affect the theorizing in social sciences in India? In other words, what is the relationship between quest for modernity in India, its ideological effervescence and the choice of theory? In what sense does the crisis in theory as encountered in the West is reflected also in the act of theorizing about the Indian society? Since, to deal with these issues comprehensively a fuller length and separate presentation would be necessary, I will only touch upon briefly on some of the salient issues. To begin with, we will have to deal with Indian intellectual response to modernity and theory-building as a historical process. This response was mediated through western colonial contact in which symmetry of communicative interaction was, right from the beginning, tinged with auora of domination and exploitation by a foreign power representing an alien civilization. The ideology of disenchantment felt by the Indian intellectuals, therefore, was enmeshed in a thick web of ambiguity and ambivalence. This is also reflected in the writings of most of our sociologists. Radha Kamal Mukherjee, who among the few sociologists in India undertook the effort towards a systematic and formal construction of a general theory of society, not only criticizes but rejects the Enlightenment ideology of modernity. Enlightenment ideology, as we know, the building block of the western social science theorizing and constitutes the sum total of the notion of disenchantment. In the western context, disenchantment is a process which leads to secularization and rationalisation of the people's worldview and their normative perspective on the life-world. By this process humans are liberated (alienated) from the "great chain of being" which bound man in sacred-mystical relationship of hierarchy and transcendence with the Godhead. Radha Kamal Mukherjee, on the other hand, posits the view that a general theory of society cannot be formulated withou anchoring, society within a triad of 'Man-God-Nature' configuration. For this, it would be essential to move away from the ideology of disenchantment to a position where science ceases to be neutral to moral values, where rationality is defined not pragmatically as utilitarianism but it is located in ethical primacy. In India, we find it in the Buddhist notion of *karuna* or compassion and the Vedantic concept of "universal humanism". Even, in early sixties, Mukherjee had anticipated the endemic crisis in the western social science, and its projects of modernity, industrialism and utilitarian praxis. He commented extensively on the moral challenges faced by the western civilization and forewarned Indian intellectuals regarding mimetic espousal of its cause. We continually find this perspective echoed in many subsequent contributions of Indian sociologists dealing with the themes of tradition and modernization and science and human values.

Indeed, western contact at the levels of intellectual and social sciences in India have deeply influenced not only its methodology but in most cases the choices of the substantive areas for study. Nevertheless, such influence, has remained self-limiting in character for two reasons: first, because there has largely existed an alienative relationship between the western philosophy of enlightenment and the Indian philosophical traditions, systems of beliefs and values; and secondly, because very few Indian sociologists and social scientists have attempted constructing 'grand sociological theories', particularly those having a nomological orientation. For example, we witness continual attempts by social scientists in our country to Indianize Marxism, less so philosophically but more in the process of its operationalization. We also witness attempts to integrate dialectical materialist philosophy of Marxism with the Indian atheistic and materialistic philosophical traditions. This has been going on in our social sciences together with the quest for alternate orientations. The same is true for those who reject the basic premises of Marxism and its variants. When once I tried to scrutinize elements of functional theory which is widely acclaimed to have influenced most writings of sociologists or social anthropologists in their studies of villages, urban communities, tribes and various societal problems in India, I found no logical or nomological basis for such a conclusion. I found, uses of various persuasions of theory in most social science writings in India either with inter-paradigmatic mixes or their uses in metaphorical terms (Singh, 1998; 1986). The uses of theory in the writings of our social scientists remain mostly at the 'a-theoretic' level with extensive usages of conceptual schemes where the emphasis upon the indigenous content in operationalization of concepts is very strong.

Therefore, the logic of disenchantment in theory that has severely fractured western sociology and social sciences, has not affected Indian social sciences. Cynics may attribute it to the lack of our theoretic development. Such conclusion may be seriously flawed. The root of our muted or adaptive response to disenchantment rests with our collective cultural consciousness and the way we have responded to modernization. There are a number of studies which reveal the capacity of our native traditions and institutions to respond adaptively to the disenchantment ideology of modernization. Charles Taylor (1991), in his book, *The Ethic of Authenticity*, aptly describes the main elements of western disenchantment ideology of modernization to comprise three attributes or its 'malaises'. These are: first, worries resulting from individualism; secondly, anxieties caused by the 'primacy of instrumental reason' which results in mindless celebration of technology; and third, the political consequences of individualism and primacy of instrumental reason which Alexis de Tocqeville described as "soft despotism". It may prevail in a welfare state and also in nation-states in the web of globalization. From these three characteristics three basic consequences emerge which bedevil the western civilization today. Taylor writes: "The first fear is about what we might call a loss of meaning, the fading of moral horizons. The second concerns the eclipse of ends, in the face of rampant instrumental reason. And, the third is about a loss of freedom" (1991: 10). The question is: how have Indian people's values and social structure been affected by these malaises of modernity? As revealed by numerous studies in India, we find that values of instrumentalism which trigger technological adaption have indeed penetrated our life-world. But, the level at which individualism and the 'soft-state' affect western life-world have not yet permeated in our society. This may largely be due to the rudimentary level of industrialization and urbanization of our society or may be it results from our cultural resilience gained through millennia old history of cultural and social encounters with the alien civilizations ! It may also be due to the primacy of values in our life not as means to an end but as an end itself !

These conditions have delimited the scope of tensions at the level of social theory in our case despite the challenges of disenchantment ideology of modernization. It remains an open question, however, as to what would be the ultimate level of equilibrium that Indian tradition would be able to evolve in its adaptive response to the modernization and disenchantment, as logical, moral and social issues of tomorrow !

COMMUNITY AND ETHNICITY

The contemporary global social situation is confronted with a paradox. The traditional community organizations are under acute moral, social and economic pressure and in most cases facing decline. The phenomenon of ethnicity, on the other hand, shows a remarkable rise in strength in terms of social organization, moral legitimation, consciousness and movement. This paradox in the emergent contemporary social processes owes much to the logic of disenchantment ideology. In the post-industrial western societies, the dilemmas of modernity are reflected in the feeling of alienation of the individual which itself is a consequence of self-indulgent individualism. This is further reinforced by the decay of community life and community sentiments mainly due to the overwhelming growth of the mass society anchored on television, Internet, telephony and other electronic instruments of communication. Family too is undergoing basic transformation as a social institution and as a jural entity with phenomenal rise in the incipience of conjugal living out of wedlock. In western societies it is posing new problems for legal and welfare policies of family, child care and gender rights.

These development coincide with growth in the feeling of ethnicity. Ethnicity at its root lies in the consciousness of identity and cultural self-awareness of a community or communities which share a common political and economic destiny. The processes through which communities transform themselves into ethnic group may be many, such as a minority status due to migration to other countries, acute consciousness of alienation due to exploitation within their own country of residence as for example, due to uneven levels of developmental opportunities. This feeling which is rooted essentially in existential deprivation of ethnic groups in relation to the dominant communities is sharpened by projection of deprivations into symbolic idiom of politics. This idiom of politics has more recently become the official ideology of development, particularly explicated by the World Summit on Development held in Copenhagen in early 1990s. The notion of development has thus inextricably got linked with human rights of the minorities, displaced persons, children, women and other vulnerable sections of society. Ethnicity, therefore, is an ideology and social process which is essentially political in nature. Its origin lies in the ideology of modernity which permeates its entire symbolic and social structural formation. It may not be out of place to submit a proposition that ethnicity as a social and cultural phenomenon is a child of the logic of disenchantment in the life-world. Ethnicity is, therefore, essentially a political and a modern phenomenon. Traditional societies did have communities based on the territorial and emotional bonds of togetherness and unity of sentiments. They also, from time to time, entered into conflict with other communities defined as alien in terms of kinship, brotherhood or territory etc. But such communities were rarely ethnicized. In other words, the demands they made or projects they outlined for themselves were symbolically not entrenched in the notions of human rights, liberty and political and cultural identity or separatism etc., all of which as ideologies are product of the modern civilization and its political symbolic paradigm.

When we look at the Indian social situation from the above perspective, we find that forces of modernization have brought about two different kinds of processes into full play. First, there is growth of ethnicity, where each movement articulates a definitive cultural and political agenda of autonomy and identity. This applies to most of the ethnic movements in the north-eastern parts of our country. We also have ethnic movements resulting from political-religious persecution of a section of our people resulting from their physical displacement. The case of the Pundits of Kashmir belongs to this category despite its uniqueness in many other ways. One instance of uniqueness is that Pundits are Hindus, the majority religious group of India, and yet their status today is that of a cultural and social minority forcibly evicted from their homeland by forces of terrorism and religious fundamentalism. In my opinion religious fundamentalism and its terrorist and other activistic manifestations have little to do with religion as such. Their phenomenology is rooted in politics by means of political violence. Religious fundamentalism, in this sense, is a modern phenomenon. It is totally alienated from the traditional worldview of religion and its life-world. It ethnicizes religion and qualitatively disenchants religious values and practices robbing them of their traditional communitarian values of piety and brotherhood, which constitute the basis for cultural and religious pluralism in societies.

There is a global trend towards the breakdown of communitarianism and community values. It is also reflected in contemporary India. Here, it is not so much a product of post-industrialization. It is, on the other hand, a consequence of overpoliticization without accompaniments of the material benefits that a post-industrial society offers to its citizens. In 1950s when sociologists were studying the villages in India, their focus on social structure, values and forces of social change did in most cases revealed some evidence of community solidarity in rural society. They made a distinction between caste and class on the basis of a premise that caste constituted a system of interdependent organic solidarity based on ritual, economic and social reciprocity. Class, as a system, on the other hand, was held to comprise units in mutual relationships of competition or even conflict. This in case of castes applies no longer today in most of our villages. Inter-caste relationships have become acutely conflictual and as a result of it the semblance of community solidarity that did continually express in the past has almost been totally broken down. Most village communities have now become political communities, and each caste group in a village attempts consolidation of its interests in an outer-directed fashion in association with similar caste groups outside the village. When it becomes an organized institutional process, it results into the formation of the caste associations. These associations, however, do not offer the full advantages of associative interest groups as in the industrial-democratic societies which from Alexis Tocquville to Raymond Aron have described. This is because in caste associations the location of interests or socio-economic or political objectives is placed within the relationships of primordiality which is not only narrow but without a stable base. The history of caste associations in India and caste-based political affiliations offers concrete evidence of the ever changing membership loyalties like shifting sand. This nullifies the thesis that caste-based mobilization can form the basis for India's modernization or that caste in India may perform the modernizing functions of associative groups.

The social structural impediment, that the Indian society is confronted with today, is the lack of secular rational principles of membership based on the unity of cultural, social, political and economic interests to form associative groups which could effectively mediate between the state and the people for realization of goals and redressal of grievances. This aspect of social change which has the potential to logically culminate in the augmentation of the civil rights movements, is very weak in India. The caste and the ethnic principles of social and political mobilization, despite their relevance in selected spheres of demand and protest, cannot reach up to the level where realization of broad and effective consensus of the entire categories of deprived people or those victimized by the structures of domination such as the state, business corporations, media barons, etc., can be established.

The rise in ethnic movements and new social movements related to ecology, gender and human rights, etc., results from the heartless manner in which the operative structures of domination is society, such as the state, corporations and multinationals, encroach upon the rights of the weak and vulnerable sections of society. In this regard, the situation in India presents a complex scenario. Here, we witness a cleavage between the cultural and existential agendas in ethnic movements. The existential agenda, which forms a part of their political, economic and social demands, seems to be defined by the logic of modernity having resonance of disenchantment ideology. But, the cultural agenda in several ethnic movements, particularly those based on religious affiliation, often tends to be anchored on narrow fundamentalism. From this, yet another contradiction emerges. Most ethnic movements rationalize their agenda through the sanctity of cultural pluralism disregarding the contradiction between fundamentalism and cultural pluralism as ideologies. Janus-like ethnicity has two faces: one mirrors the values of self-consciousness quite in tune with the logic of disenchantment and the other tends to foreclose dialogue with other cultures which is an anti-thesis of modernity. Communalism in India that sponsors several ethnic movements has this character.

POLITICAL IDEOLOGY, DEMOCRACY AND THE STATE

The crisis of modernity also permeates the political ideology and the institutions of democracy and nation-state. The tradition of liberalism, civic culture and industrial capitalism were products of two revolutions---one industrial and the other republican. Ideologies of both converged on the notion of disenchantment. Today, however, both institutions of democracy and state are considered flawed by intellectuals and thinking public in most of the developed world. There is widespread feeling of uneasiness about corporatization of governance, rise in technocracy without responsibility, erosion in the quality of leadership, its non-accountability and the looming erosion in the sovereignty of state itself. The logic of disenchantment which had led to the ascendance of technology, to a cyber-society or the upcoming information society, has ceased to inform. It lacks transparency. The mega-structures of media and communication, with global speed and invisible controls, tend to reduce human being to an abstraction or a digital number and take away from the nation-state the effective power to intervene. This nurtures a diffuse feeling among the citizens of the loss of identity of an authentic self. The globalization of communication is reinforced by free-floating power of multinational economic corporations to defy national boundaries.

The dissatisfaction thus engendered has led intellectuals in the developed nations to search for alternate political models of governance. They pine for 'reinventing democracy'. A time-bound electoral verdict of five or six years interregnum is found to promote lack of accountability in the leaders during the entire interim duration. The need is felt for reform in civil institutions such as the citizen's monitoring bodies, public auditing of elected leadership in terms of performance and accountability with right to recall, and greater empowerment of political organizations at the local level etc. These developments are symptomatic of the flaws in the institution of governance in contemporary industrialized nations. The point to note is that in the process of technological and economic development the essential objectives of democratic form of governance, that were anchored on the values of freedom, equality and brotherhood of citizenship, do not seem to have been realized. All these values seem to have been compromised due to the ascendance of corporatized technocratic culture in governance. Citizens feel least empowered to comprehend the process of decision-making much less are they in the position to intervene.

The crisis of democracy and state is not of much less proportion in our own country. Our problem is not so much of corporatization or technocracy as that of institutionalization of civil values and democratic institutions themselves. Appeals to caste, ethnicity and localism have not allowed the concept of citizenship to come to the foreground in Indian politics. The mediating social and cultural forces of non-democratic character continually impinge upon the formation of political parties, their political and social agenda and mode of performance. The civil institutions have not yet evolved, and where they exist their performance is limited in nature. The process of democracy is yet to evolve a truly secular and representative character. These lacunas may be due to underdevelopments in the field of economy, education and social justice. Or it may be a forerunner to a new blend of social and cultural practices in the constitution of democracy as a process of self-governance. It is clear, however, there is a gathering perception of uneasiness in India about the effectiveness of the current form of democracy to throw up a leadership committed to values and practices of a responsible and responsive governance. The ideology of disenchantment, therefore, seems to have had a limited yet fractured role in the formation of the Indian democracy and the nation-state.

DISENCHANTMENT VERSUS REENCHANTMENT

The dilemma of modernity self-evidently is of many hues. It is also multidimensional. Some philosophers and sociologists in the developed world have proposed solutions. Others have shown pessimism, depending on their judgment of the nature and potential of the modern instrumental society. Ernest Gellner feels that solution to the crisis of modernity in the western society will emerge from the evolutionary process of the disenchantment ideology itself. In other words, the social pathology of post-industrial society could be overcome with strengthening the meaningfulness of leisure time, rescheduling of work and employment, redefining the role of education in society and by increasing the empowerment of individual rights through voluntary civic institutions.

Charles Taylor seeks the solution in the ethic of authenticity and the primacy of *dialogue* in the sphere of human relationships by enriching "the self-affirming freedom of the individuals". Habermas anticipates that possible solution may rest in a social and cultural agenda of legitimation which strengthens communicative interaction. All these and other similar solutions bypass the issue of moral autonomy. The question is: what autonomy will the moral values or normative principles in human acts of choice making would enjoy in a modern society? Will it remain at the level of 'ethic of benevolence' which merely ensures a certain quality of material life and pleasure ensured in a modern instrumental society or would it also have a space for an autonomous moral standard? This dilemma of modern society is no where near solution.

The ideology of pluralism has a place of deeper sociological significance at this level. As I have proposed earlier, moral values cannot be totally relativized, even though a large part of our values fall within the domain of instrumental or utilitarian reason. Dialogical communities of human beings are, therefore, endowed with values which are *expressive* or original and those which are instrumental in nature. At the first level, societies are constituted by cultural pluralism each pursuing relatively autonomous normative paths. At the instrumental level, however, commonalities between societies and groups must also be envisaged through which dialogue and consensus at a broader level of social, economic and political infraction is made possible. Human beings live in the symbolic universe of languages which endow dialogue with two significant levels of meanings: first, local level of community, ethnicity or other primary social groupings; and secondly, dialogue also inheres symbolic exchange of meanings at a much extensive level where rational or instrumental values do not particularize meanings but tend essentially to universalize it. We have, for instance, a universal language of science and certain forms of art and culture belonging to this category.

Solution to the crisis of modernity, whether in the developing or the developed world, lies in recognizing the dual character of our cultural and existential moorings. It necessitates recognition of cultural pluralism, strategy of consensus and reconciliation in human dealings based on dialogue and other means of communicative interactions. It also logically recognizes the need for a meaningful space within the ideology of disenchantment for values of tradition. It would be erroneous to assume that tradition as enchantment is totally fixated or it is a static category. Most prophecies get routinized over a period of time as more and more elements of their constitutive values cease to remain transcendental or supra-rational. They pass into the realm of rational or instrumental values as they seek to be more existentially rooted. A dichotomy between tradition and modernity is, therefore, untenable. What we witness in real life is an interactive or adaptive relationship between the two. Therefore, the crisis of disenchantment cannot be resolved by a swing from disenchantment from modernity to enchantment with tradition, but by establishing an interactive relationship between modernity and tradition within the frame of the ideology of pluralism.

References

Cassierer, E., *Philosophy of Symbolic Forms*, Vol.2, New Haven: Yale University Press, 1966.

Gellner, E., *Culture Identity and Politics*, Cambridge: Cambridge University Press, 1987.

---, *Reason and Culture*, Oxford: Bookwell, 1992.

Taylor, C., *The Ethic of Authenticity*, Canada: Canadian Broadcasting Corporation, 1991.

Singh, Yogendra, *Image of Man: Ideology and Theory in Indian Sociology*, Delhi: Chanakya Press, 1998.

---, *Indian Sociology: Social Conditioning and Emerging Concerns*, Delhi, Vistaar Publishers, 1986.

Vattimo, G., *The Transparent Society*, Oxford: Polity Press, 1992.

9

Community, Change and Alienation

During the fifty years of independence, many changes that have happened in our society can be a source of satisfaction. Yet, the feelings of regrets and lost opportunities remain. Not only persistent poverty and illiteracy cause dismay but the continued growth of communalism, rapid erosion of moral and civic values, and the decline in family solidarity threatening its role in providing succourance to children, women and the aged, are matters of deep concern. We have increased conflict in society on account of the negative demonstration effects of fragmented development in the fortunes of classes, communities and regions. In our evaluation of these issues we have so far used parameters of economy, ethnicity, caste-class and social ecology (rural-urban processes). We have not paid attention to the role of community. As a primordial social structure it occupies a place of utmost significance for understanding and perhaps resolving most of our social problems.

Community like family and kin group is the basic institution of human society. Both institutions have suffered serious onslaughts to their existence from the forces released by new ideologies and techno-industrial advancement. Yet, these institutions have survived though not in the original form. Today, there is increased recognition of their vital significance for the well being of human society. The West, which in the early phases of the industrial revolution celebrated individualism and the sonsequent end of community, now so much as pines for its revival. Anchored as it was on intimate person to person relationships in local settings and bonds of human reciprocity and solidarity, the replacement of community by contractual market-oriented relationships has not augmented the quality of life. After gathering about four centuries of fruits of industrialization and modernization, the West is making strident demands for restoration of community values and strengthening of the institution of family.

Increased emphasis on individualism, consumerism, contract and market relationship jeopardized the family and community values. This increased the alienation of individuals first from these basic institutions and later on from their own self-identity. To describe it the scientists coined apt metaphors of "lonely men" moving in "lonely crowds". Now, there is intense disenchantment from such paradigms of industrialization and development. There is a new quest for the restoration of values and bonds of community and family. The problem in the West is of how to restore these institutions in society after having destroyed the foundations on which they were anchored. There is no solution of this even in the post-industrial society. The post-modern information society can only promise interaction with a cyber-community through the Internet.

THE INDIAN EXPERIENCE

Our experience in India is historically different. The forces of contract, industrialism and market have not been so pervasive or strong here as in the West. In our case politics has done to community structure and its relationship what industrialism and market did to this institution in the West. Community, as a social institution as it existed in the past, has been converted into a political institution. Consequently, here too very much like in the West, the solitary and integrative functions of community which provided safeguard in the situations of stress and conflict to the weaker members such as the women, the destitute, the elderly and the children within society have weakened or withered away. Communities are imbued with feelings of factiousness, social disharmony and mutual alienation.

The phenomenon of alienation in our society is also becoming worrisome, both at the individual and inter-group levels. In the western society, the pangs of social alienation are minimized by the presence of compensatory mechanisms of strong institutionalized relationships with the civic society. However, alienation is endemic at the level of the individual. In our case, the civic society has yet to gain strength, expand its scope and get institutionalized. Hence, the incidence of individual alienation as measured by the number of drifters, chronic unemployed and rejected such as the widows, the elderly and other marginalized individuals is increasing. The dimension of social alienation in our society is evident from the growing incidence of communal conflict, caste and ethnic tensions and violent movements by marginalized groups such as the *dalits*, the dispossessed and the rural poor.

A close relationship, for example, between the levels of disintegration of the traditional community structure and values and increase in communal tensions, has been widely noticed. Communal conflict largely continues to be an urban problem as the urban setting provides the optimal measure of decline in community values and relationship. Traditionally, both rural and urban centres used to have strong institutionalized community organizations and reciprocity of human relationships. As the studies of the pre-industrial Indian cities and of its villages have revealed, the *jajmani* system, caste and village *panchayats* in the villages and the artisans and other functionary guilds or *panchayats* in cities maintained the strength of community harmony.

These supervised the norms of family relationships and saw

to it that the social obligations were adhered to by individuals and groups. This pattern largely continued well upto the early phases of the British rule in our country. It soon began to decline as the new economic policies of the British regime contributed to the disintegration of the traditional economy. Also, the colonial administrative structure began to render many old institutions at the community level ineffective or even redundant.

Politicalization of community relations soon followed. First, it started with the caste. The census operations based on the caste enumeration imparted legitimacy to independent caste identity and alienated it from the community obligations for the first time. The principle of segmentation was enhanced at the cost of inter-caste or community relationships. Moreover, the census operations being sponsored by the state gave a political legitimation to the institution of caste. After independence, the caste-based census stopped but the politicization of caste never ceased. It continued the process of alienating the community bonds. The communalization of religious and tribal groups also followed. The politics after independence turned into the sectarian politics. It has played havoc with our traditionally strong community bonds. These bonds held inter-caste, inter-religious and inter-ethnic relationships organically integrated. In situations of conflicts these community bonds served as mechanisms of regulation and reconciliation.

With the march of new forces of industrialization, urbanization and globalization of cultures and economy, the disintegrative pressures upon the community structure are increasing day by day. Similar experience in the West, which has led to socially disastrous consequences, has also led to serious rethinking on the paradigms of development. Focus has shifted from abstract mega institutions or mega projects of development to smaller, concrete, pluralistic and humanly interactive institutions and projects of development. Instead of market relations subordinating human bonds, now it is the human interactive dimension which is recognized as the pre-eminent element in the institutional facets of economic, organizational and social development. The legitimacy and identity of the local, ethnic, communitarian and small have been recognized. We have to draw our lessons from this and be forewarned.

FUTURE OF COMMUNITY

How will the community fare in this process? It is obvious that serious damage to this institution has already been done. We are no exception, even though we are largely a rural society. Despite the recognition of the sustainable and human dimensions in the new models of development, the forces of post-industrial transformation make it impossible to restore back the damaged community structures and relationships on the traditional pattern. The western philosophers did recognize the nature of loss that industrialism was anticipated to perpetrate upon society due to the disintegration of community. They thought of the utopian communities, communist society and religious brotherhood, etc., from time to time as remedies to the problems of human alienation and social amorality of the market-oriented industrial society. None of these alternatives have, however, survived or have proved to be socially viable. One major reason for their failure was that most these communities were conceptualized outside or even in opposition to the institution of civic society.

We have to recognize the supreme importance of the values and social institutions of the civic society for the better contemporary and future destiny of humankind. Historically, community structures pre-date the evolution of civic society, and seem to have suffered decay as the civic society has advanced or expanded. Should we, therefore, assume an inevitable antinomy between community and civic society? Obviously, it need not be so. The antinomy is more apparent than real. It has also resulted from faulty application of the instruments of techno-economic development. These have neglected or even destroyed the role of the human inter-active forces. A void has thus been created. Consequently, the civic society tends to be increasingly de-humanized. The likely way-out seems to be the establishment of the institutions and associations which perform the functions of community, even when its members are governed by the rules of the civic society. The two institutions, viz., the community and the civic society, may have to be strengthened to reinforce each other rather than be mutual rivals.

Such surrogate communities will have to be organized as a conscious effort towards the strengthening both of the foundation of the civic society and its instruments of techno-economic and organizational advancement. This should imply that voluntary self-organizations based on the promotion of a variety of social, cultural, religious and ethnic interests are promoted. These will operate essentially within a decentralized, local, concrete and human interactive boundary. Such community organizations should not arise out of the disenchantment from or opposition to the civic society, but as its organic supplement. Its membership may be defined by the commonality of interests which may not necessarily be unimodal or specific as in an association or a club but diffuse and inclusive as in a community. Community's objectives should be laid out to perform a variety of functions and look after a set of interests ranging from the personal to the familial and the communitarian. Unlike the traditional communities of the past, however, the new communities would have to be consciously organized on a voluntary basis. It would link the processes of mega market-oriented forces of change with those that are local and communitarian. It would also link the community with the civic society thus minimizing the cost of social change and alienation.

10

Leisure and Social Change

Emerging Issues in India

It is curious to note that sociology of leisure forms a neglected area of sociological research in India. The reason for this probably rests in the social conditioning of priorities of research and historical development of our society. We had to fight for our freedom from a colonial regime and from institutional and cultural malpractices within our society to construct a project for our future. In this process sociology orientated itself more closely to issues of social, economic, political and cultural developments. It focussed on studies of villages, castes, tribes and on processes of their change and continuity. Cultural sociology, which could have had closer affinity with studies of leisure, also had its priorities determined rather historically. The national movement, need to articulate principles of national unity, the urge to contest distorted western portraits of Indian culture, and society which enlarged *centrifugal tensions* to the neglect of *centripetal linkages* of society were more urgent. It became necessary to look at culture from the perspective of linkages rather than identities. The sociologists, social scientists and public men found it imperative to analyze cultural features, styles and forms in their varieties of cultural traditions to articulate national identity.

Consequently, studies of leisure, sociology of time, fashions, styles, media forms, communication systems, art, aesthetics and literature etc., which have been widely researched in the West, have only haltingly started in India. This is evident from the trend reports on sociological researches composed together under the auspices of the Indian Council of Social Science Research. It seems that sociology in India is now at a new turning point. The processes of change during the past four decades have set into motion social, cultural and economic forces that make it imperative for sociologists and social scientists to examine closely the relationships among factors like work, social structure, ecology and cultural styles. Sociology of leisure constitutes a vital element in this matrix.

Sociological studies are located in a paradigm of thought and methods which emerged historically through the rise of societal self-awareness. This was made possible by the Enlightenment ideology of equality, freedom and human brotherhood—a unique contribution to humanity. When we talk of leisure and social change we may have to identify the phases of social transformation before and after this historical revolution in ideology. It is intrinsically related to the patterns of leisure, work, cultural styles and social and techno-economic structures of society.

PATTERNS OF LEISURE IN TRADITIONAL INDIAN SOCIETY

It would be simplistic to talk of the pattern of leisure in the singular even for the traditional Indian society. This society had its own periodic phases of cultural and structural differentiations. Instead of one there were many *traditional* patterns in society. Nevertheless, one could heuristically talk of certain common elements in the traditional society of India which contributed to the patterning of leisure. Cultural ideology and social structure of this society closely defined leisure activities.

Ideologically, the concepts of time and history as they shaped the definition of self and society also influenced the notions of leisure and work. All traditional societies, even simpler ones, had their own cosmology and metaphysics of time, birth and rebirth which patterned their rythms of work and leisure. Sacred and profane, pragmatic and transcendental, utilitarian and non-utilitarian levels of symbolization of work deeply influenced their perception of leisure and leisure time. The notion of leisure in states of being and becoming as creative self-affirmation possibly emanates from this metaphysical dualism of time and work.

Modes of production, technology and division of labour, caste and class played important roles in patterning of leisure. The division between agrarian and industrial modes of production in traditional India contributed to social differentiation and forms of leisure. The commercial, cultural and political linkages among villages, small towns and capital cities articulated these patterns of leisure in different but interrelated forms. The overall distinction was between folk and the elite forms of leisure and work. The slow pace of technological innovations gave a measure of continuity to these forms. The folk pattern was located in oral traditions of culture. The elite tradition was manifested in the written textual forms. This distinction was, however, partial as many overlaps between the two patterns in the concrete situation existed, such as the family, the brotherhood and the community. The folk and elite forms of leisure were socially manifested in the lifestyles, culture and work patterns of peasants, petty artisans and labourers on the one hand and the merchants, literati and feudal lords on the other. The distinctive feature of leisure in traditional society was probably its organic communitarian character, its integration with work and its ritualization at selected levels of manifestation. Its deeper linkages with ecology and modes of production were reflected in its patterning on calendaric rythms and life-cycle rituals.

The relationship between leisure and work, gender, community and social stratification had indeed evolved an orderly pattern. The hierarchical principle of ordering of economic and social relationships also operated in the domain of leisure activities. The patronage to several forms of leisure activities such as dance dramas, Ram Lila, Krishna Lila, musical meets and a variety of ceremonies which served as leisure time activities was given by the feudal nobility or local *zamindars* (landlords). The village temple, the seat of many artistic and cultural festivities, was under their control. In other parts, the entire community or panchayat exercised this control. Leisure, as a behavioural and cultural phenomenon, was not entirely dissociated from community life or its repretoire of social sanctions. Leisure with the exception of some institutional manifestation was also not dissociated from work. It was common in traditional society for people to go to work and combine with work their expressive leisurely urges, individually and collectively, randomly and in stylized forms. This was particularly so in villages on the occasions of sowing, harvesting, threshing and disposal of crops. The village *chaupals* or urban street-corners were men and women came together to exchange notes, to gossip, to sing and celebrate, and also to complete work, such as weaving, knitting, basket-making and other types of jobs. The village wells or ponds were celebrated places for women to combine work with leisure. The alienation of work from leisure results from breakdown of the traditional society and its worldview. This should not mean that in traditional society no domains of leisure dissociated from work existed. Such domains, however, had their place among the privileged class of society.

This pattern of leisure held sway for centuries in India due to stagnation of modes of production, technology and social organization of society. The technology of production, communication and transport remained unchanged over a long period of time maintaining the old pattern of leisure. This began to change with India's encounter with modern industrial society during the colonial and independent phases of development. New processes initiated during the freedom movement were consolidated after independence.

EMERGING PATTERNS OF LEISURE

This emerging pattern of leisure is deeply influenced by changes in social structure, economy, technology and cultural and political processes in society. Significant social and economic changes were initiated in the traditional society soon after independence. Caste-based village panchayats were abolished, land reforms were introduced abolishing feudalism, *zamindari* and intermediaries. Adult franchise was introduced for national local elections. New technologies, both in sectoral and institutional terms, were brought in for improvement of agriculture and industry. The print and electronic media, which had a halting start during the colonial period, got massive fillip after independence. These emerged as a strong arm for diffusion and orchestration of information, cultural symbols and recreational packages of various kinds. The political processes of democratic participation set into motion among social groups such as classes, castes, tribes and ethnic groups new movements for consolidation of consciousness. Its emergence has radically, though not wholly, disturbed the traditional pattern of leisure and leisure institutions in society.

In rural India which constitutes the dominant segment of society, introduction of land reforms and new technology in agriculture has triggered a process of social restructuration. Modern agriculture dictates its own time-schedule independent of traditional calendaric cycle of work and leisure. It has thus rendered traditional work codes in agriculture redundant. The oral saying encoding rules of agricultural work cycle have been replaced by a work schedule determined by science laboratory, irrigation technology and market forces. The new agriculture which has ushered in 'green revolution' in India robs people of their old styles of work-leisure relationships and its ritualization. It also displaces several categories of workers, especially women, older folk and children, froin traditional roles in agriculture. Thus, the communitarian participation in agriculture has been increasingly segmentized. Market has penetrated where once community used to rule. The urban-rural nexus has become stronger and in a new qualitative form, not for participation in a common worldview at different but compatible levels as in the past, but as arenas of market, behaviour, bargain for resources and shelter for migration.

The abolition of feudalism and the decline in the role of religious literati have caused the decay of many leisurely pursuits which were patronized by these classes. In some regions village councils keep a few of them going. The role of village *chaupals*, community wells, temples or other sacred or cultural places has been weakening due to penetration of mass media, cinema and video system of entertainment. The communities which made a living by entertaining people by dances, dramas, acrobatics, mimes or other recreational activities are fast losing their vocation. On festive occasions such as marriage, birth or social festivities, videos are replacing these traditional entertainers. The *chaupals* are being replaced by roadside tea-stalls where people assemble to supplement their tea with newspaper information, gossips, and exchange of notes with local and outside members. The institutionalized etiquette of *chaupal* has disappeared in the random mode of behaviour at the tea-stall.

These changes have introduced new dimensions to the rural pattern of leisure and its mode of work. Institutionalized forms of culture to which leisure in the past was orientated, is now increasingly exposed to forces of what is known as 'mass culture' or 'popular culture'. This is happening both at the rural and urban settings of our society. In rural society, this process is reinforced by disenchantment from village life. The green revolution has not only altered the social coordinates of leisure, but it has also sharpened the consciousness of social inequality and raised the level of aspiration. The emerging changes being non-egalitarian and ideologically conservative, large sections of rural working classes, artisans and youth are feeling alienated from village economy and its cultural and social institutions. This has led to massive migration of rural folk from villages to cities and metropolises across the country. Depending on regional characteristics, this migration is also to foreign lands, such as the Gulf countries, Europe and North America. Increasing intensity of migration has introduced heterogeneity in lifestyle and patterns of leisure.

The relationship between migration and leisure has to be analyzed at several levels of social stratification. There is massive migration from rural to urban centres mainly of the working classes or rural poor. The migration to foreign lands has socially a more differentiated character, being of the artisan and lower middle classes to the Gulf nations and of middle and upper classes to Europe and North America. There is also a degree of ethnic selectively in this process. A new form of internal migration within the rural region itself is also taking place in some parts of the country, mainly of the agricultural labourers who go from place to place in search of contract labour in agriculture. This movement of population, together with growing volume of internal and foreign tourism, has extended the process of social restructuration to the domains of leisure and style of life.

These changes also coincide with other developments in society. Rise of entrepreneurial, professional and mercantile classes, enlargement of administrative, political and cultural elites, etc., set new standards for leisure time activities. These sections also selectively incorporate alien elements of leisure and culture which has demonstration effect on the style of life. It affects culture and leisure in our country due to their social and economic domination over society. More than 150 million members of the middle and upper classes in India have generated a new market for print and electronic media entertainment and a high profile consumerist lifestyle. A small section among these also resembles what Veblen has called "a leisure class indulging in conspicuous consumption and waste".

The forces of social mobility, migration, class restructuration and intensity of culture contacts, from within and outside the country, have resulted in changes in the pattern of leisure. The motor forces for this comes from the market forces and capitalist mode of production. This process acquires a new edge due to high rate of population growth in society. It raises the proportion of the youth in society being intensely motivated towards new orientations in leisure and recreation. However, these changes introduce several contradictory tendencies in the forms of leisure. The traditional pattern still subsists even though changes have begun to take place in the form and functions of leisure. Increasingly, radio, television, videos, audio, magazines and newspapers are eroding the interpersonal communitarian mode of communication and leisure. Due to expansion of market forces, a large part of artifacts, symbols, styles and forms related to traditional leisure and recreational pattern, are being incorporated in the mass media forms. A class of 'culture entrepreneurs' has emerged which undertakes systematic marketing of leisure and culture goods within the country and outside. It encourages new waves in fashion and lifestyle such as emphasis on ethnic designs, artifacts and instruments of leisure. Tourism from abroad, both of foreigners and non-resident Indians, reinforces this process.

The cultural base of these changes exists in values of utilitariansim, acquisitiveness, individualistic rationalism and quest for pleasure. When translated into leisure behaviour it tends to deviate basically from the worldview of society and leisure as envisaged by our nation. Elements of humanism, free self-expression, participatory communication, institutionalized collective sharing and participation, or in other words, the social and human character of leisure is eroded by these developments. The symbiotic relationship between work and leisure is gone. It is replaced by more individualized, hedonistic and alienative relationship between leisure and work. The person is replaced by audience. The way for the emergence of a mass culture or popular culture with commensurate forms of leisure is ensured. Leisure ceases to be a mode of self-expression, self-affirmation and celebration of universal human consciousness. It becomes a commodity or is subjectively reified as something to be acquired or maximized. Instead of affirmation of one's humanity, leisure becomes a distinctive mark of consumption and social domination.

The indicators of social and economic development in our society have this dual character. On the one hand, there is growth in technological and material base of society, there is more prosperity, less desease or deprivation for a growing section of population. On the other hand, there is poverty, deprivation and disease. Serious value displacements are therefore generated by the rise of the new acquisitive class. The dualism between the rich and poor, traditional and contemporary and communitarian and alienative modes of leisure get sharpened. These generate a social as well as a cultural crisis in society. Even though traditional forms of leisure continue to persist or have worked out adaptive changes, yet, in more crucial areas of leisure, the alienative forms are growing strong. Despite efforts to establish academies of art, culture and theatre, the progress made towards creative integration remains feeble. Their growth potential in encapsulated by the interests of the urban, industrial and professional elite. In the rural areas where about 70 per cent of our people live, the folk theatre groups, the artists and traditional entertainers are being rapidly displaced and impoverished by new agrarian developments and social transformation.

The mass media, particularly the television which is rapidly penetrating the domains of leisure, are envisaged to project images of person, culture and society to reinforce humanistic social and economic development of society. Its symbols and messages are expected to help in developing a modern, just, prosperous and harmonious society. The richer elements of India's traditional heritages drawn from all regions, communities and groups are to be articulated to show their ever-lasting relevance. Despite there being some evidence that these objectives remain on the agenda of television, the encroachment of consumerist values and market culture in its programmes generates scepticism. It is evident that uneven social development has enhanced the power of the rich to control the institution of mass culture and its pattern of leisure. Relying heavily on mass media for promotion of leisure would logically mean increasing the control of these classes on leisure and culture of society. It would threaten and rupture the cultural and social objectives of modernization of our society.

An important problem in evolving a policy on leisure and its institutional pattern in India relates to the mix between local and cosmopolitan manifestations of culture and forms of leisure. Strange though it may appear, as the process of economic and educational development advances in a society, correspondingly there is increase in the awareness of people of their own identities as local group, ethnic, regional culture etc. Science and technology, on the one hand, promotes massificaton, homogeneization or globalization of practices and values of leisure and on the other hand, generates forces of encapsulation of consciousness in the form of localism, neo-traditionalism and fundamentalism. This problem is inevitable, particularly in India with its plural traditions. Two points may be recognized in this context. First, localism or neo-traditionalism may not be antithetical to cosmopolitan culture if these are used as a medium of self-affirmation as a community or people. Leisure and culture in order to be meaningful social phenomena have to be rooted in community and local/regional social formations. It protects them from the onslaught of mass culture and market forces. Secondly, the localization or regionalization of cultural awareness and forms of leisure may also result from feeling of exploitation and injustice perpetrated by structures of social and economic domination. In this form, the problem assumes urgent policy dimension. It is linked with issues of promoting a just and democratic development of Indian society.

VISION OF A FUTURE SOCIETY

It is obvious that an Indian model of culture and leisure would have to be an organic part of our vision of a future society. This vision has evolved over several centuries but more concretely in courses of our national struggle for freedom. It is the vision of India as a just humanistic, prosperous and technologically and rationally progressive society. It is also a society where the dichotomy between leisure and work and work and culture is not accepted since it rejects the materialistic and alienative view of human condition. The dichotomy is not between work and leisure. It is between leisure as consumerism or leisure as communication, sharing human sociability through free expression, participation and empathy.

It is near possible that new society would be in a position to overcome problems of existential deprivations such as of hunger, shelter, illness and drudgery of work, etc. This could be achieved with the help of modern science and technology. The time lag in achieving these goals may vary depending upon the initial condition in each society, its human resources, social structure, distribution of power and reflexivity of power elite. A society even though it achieves these goals would be up against a more formidable enemy—human alienation. There is alienation even in poor society but its roots are existential. It does not totally blunt the feeling of human sociality and need for togetherness or communication. The alienation of a materially advanced society, an information society or a mass society is of a qualitatively different kind. Here, alienation is emotional, spiritual and for a person self-isolating. The culture of consumerism, mass advertising and market control of human responses robs humans of their power of communication, sociality and empathy. This also alters the meaning of leisure. Instead of being active principles of human self-expression, spontaneous communication and social participation, leisure becomes a passive experience, or a sensation to be 'enjoyed' in the isolation of one's living room. Leisure is dissociated from vital human condition.

Indian society is far from reaching this stage in near future. We are however forewarned in formulating an agenda on the future perspective on leisure. A sensitivity to this problem has been a part of our national heritage and tradition. Gandhiji and Pandit Nehru---the two architects of modern Indian society---long recognized the need for India to develop a balance between materialism and humanism. They also recognized how one-sided development may contribute to brutalization of society. A balanced development would imply not only economic growth but social justice and development of human personality, skills and sense of freedom also. An adequate economic and educational policy thus becomes organic to a relevant policy on leisure and culture.

11

Sociology and the Emerging Challenge of Change

The theme of this paper "Sociology and the Emerging Challenge of Change" articulates our collective concern. The culmination of social forces operating in our society since independence, have led us to face with many unanticipated challenges. These affect our profession as well as our society. There is a need to reflect deeply on these problems and to reorganize ourselves to meet with these challenges.

Let us first deliberate upon some of the basic challenges which confront us at present. Challenge is inherent in the process of change. It affects both individuals and societies. Its intensity, however, is governed by the nature and quality of change. The emerging forces of social change now have a qualitatively different character. These are bound to give rise to new fears and unanticipated consequences. These are *global* as well as *national* in nature. In the context of our history of colonial experiences, the term 'global' evokes anxiety in our mind. We have to examine as to how far the forces of change that are global, also bring about liberating consequences to society.

CHALLENGES OF GLOBAL FORCES

One major challenge that we encounter is a result of sudden alteration in the balance of power among nations due to the end of the cold war. It has brought about not only the need for rethinking on ideology of social change, but also triggered off cultural and social structural movements, totally out of proportion with the traditional reckoning by societies. India occupies a prominent place in this context. Ideologically, capitalism and socialism, as paradigms of social transformation, have undergone a radical shift in the estimation of both scholars and laymen. The disintegration of the USSR and changes in the policies of administration of economies in many former socialist societies, have created the myth of invincibility of capitalism as an ideology. There is economic pressure on the state to increasingly withdraw from its commitments to support many vital areas of social, economic and cultural welfare of its citizens. A plea is made to pass on such responsibilities to the free market forces, irrespective of the degree of the people's vulnerabilities. Human rights are applauded, but it does not include the citizen's right to work or measure of economic security. All over Europe and North America the state is under increasing pressure to withdraw from welfare commitments to its people. Our own society can hardly escape such pressures.

The extent to which the power of market increases and expands, the significance of the state as a supreme political institution undergoes major alterations. Idealistically, some protagonists of market even anticipate the end of the notion of sovereignty. For societies such as India, where nation-building has still not reached the level of integrative maturity, such fears of the end of sovereignty or a threat to it due to unhindered play of the global market force causes not only an acute anxiety but also poses a challenge. Ironically, the notion of a 'free market' is still a myth. Despite talk about the end of State sovereignty, the superpower role of the rich capitalist nations of the world remains intact. These nations continually hinder the rules of reciprocity in the operation of free market forces in matters of trade and transfer of technology.

It is true that the expanded role of market is organically linked with diffusion, decentralization and massification of production processes of commodities. The traditional mode of commodity production has itself undergone revolutionary changes. Increasingly, the relationship between capital and labour no longer remains as it existed in the past. The incidence of labour pursuing capital is on decline, now increasingly capital pursues labour. The cheap labour in the developing societies attracts multinational companies. These multinational companies no longer honour national boundaries, not only because of new market opportunities due to rising middle classes, but mainly due to the availability of cheap labour power. Employing the economies of scale and efficiency, the production process is decentralized and automated. Market forces released by these floating multinational concerns create new structures of interdependency between societies and cultures. They generate new forms of human resources, skills, technologies and infrastructures.

The technologies of information such as computers, satellites, mass media and telecommunications play a crucial role in the process of globalization. The space occupied by services sector in the total economy expands, and eventually turns overwhelming, in comparison with the commodity production.

The social effect of new technology is both instrumental and symbolic-intrinsic. At the instrumental level, it contributes to differentiation of occupations, roles and values which form part of a uniform global sub-culture or sub-system, and yet in the symbolic-intrinsic domain, they engender identities of self-consciousness that are segmentary or self-encapsulating. Enigmatically, the march of global society and culture carries amongst its legions the forces that reinforce smaller identities, for example, ethnicity, sub-nationalism and cultural and religious fundamentalism. Despite all its benevolent consequences, the expansion of the global domain does not resolve the problems of social and cultural alienation, conflicts due to ethnicity, and minorityism, etc. It is compounded by emergence of new social problems of disintegration of family, decline in community values and alienation of the individual.

Yet, given the nature of the contemporary technological revolution, the march of these global forces is inevitable. Each society, including our own country and our people, have to come to terms with its development. We could possibly do it in a meaningful and satisfactory manner if we evaluate this problem with a comparative historical understanding of the post-industrial phase of development of societies. We have then to place these changes in the context of our historicity.

FORCES OF SOCIAL CHANGE

Let us now look at the new challenges that forces of social change are throwing up in our society. Firstly, compared to the first two decades after independence, the social mechanisms influencing the processes of change, have undergone major transformation. The initial conditions of change in society have now qualitatively changed. Earlier, change had to be sponsored by a leadership largely thrown up during the course of the struggle for freedom. Even though, the agenda of change that evolved during the national movement, continues to draw a large measure of consensus even today, change has now ceased to be a matter of sponsorship from the top. Elements of hegemony or reconciliation which characterized earlier mechanisms for the sponsorship of social change, have now taken a new form.

This has resulted largely from both successes and failures of the policy of social change sponsored during the early decades after independence. The social and cultural base of the political leadership has now got enlarged. The fruits of democratic revolution, affirmative action in favour of the scheduled castes, scheduled tribes and backward classes, the consequences of land reforms, the Green Revolution and the massive investment through planning policies (through nationalization of banks), investment in higher education and industries, etc., have slowly contributed to a significant measure of changes in the social composition of elite, professional and administrative classes and political leadership in our society. The near monopoly of the upper castes and classes in the civic and political power in society is rapidly breaking down. Their hegemonic control on the polity has nearly ended. In other vital spheres of our social life such as the professions and industries, the pressure of change is visible. There is some evidence suggesting that a section of the middle caste, middle class peasantry in regions of Andhra Pradesh, Gujarat, Maharashtra and a few other regions of Green Revolution is slowly graduating from agriculture to trade, industries and services, marking spread of new entrepreneurship. The process is slow due to paucity of capital investment in agriculture and also due to poorer linkage between industries and agriculture. There is need for massive capital investment and modernization of technology and infrastructure. Its sociological consequences, however, are clearly visible.

These changes are triggering new responses from other sections of society as well, which are manifest at other levels of our social, economic and cultural life. Despite successes in selected areas of social and economic life, such as the expansion of the middle class social base, growth in professional and services sectors, the Green Revolution and the widening of the base of the commercial and industrial entrepreneurship etc., basic problems have remained unresolved. Nearly half of the total population is still illiterate, the rate of population growth continues to defy planned estimates though some positive trends are emerging. Poverty level is intolerably high at about 40 per cent of the total population, and the number of urban poor is increasing at a very rapid rate due to migration from villages. Multiplication of urban slums illustrates this process. The larger the city, the larger is the problem of urban poverty and its ghettoization. The discontent in the urban life is enlarged leading to continued conflicts between urban middle classes and the slum-dwelling poor. The liberalization and opening of the economy have now added a new class of the 'super-rich' and the 'neo rich' to the urban social situation. This creates among urban middle classes as well as the urban poor very complex forms of cultural, psychological and social tensions. Its significance is yet to be fully explored.

It is obvious that along with several desirable facets of social change, new social contradictions are multiplying. These encompass both our rural and urban life. The rural poor are consolidating themselves through active and aggressive movements based on caste and region. Their primordial identities, such as culture and religion, are increasingly subjected to sectarian mobilization sowing seeds of disharmony in society. The emergent peasant middle classes that enjoyed a measure of economic mobility during the 1970s and 1980s phase of the Green Revolution, are now confronted with uncertain economic future for their sons and daughters due to stagnation in agriculture, fragmentation of landholdings and poverty of capital and technology. The total result is disenchantment from rural life and the prospects that it offers to rural youth, both from the poor and middle class homes.

The intensity of this disenchantment is accentuated due to higher levels of media exposure and politicization of the younger generation. With reduction in the voting age, coupled with higher rate of population growth, particularly in the Hindi-speaking states of the northern India, we have today a very substantial population of youth who deeply and justifiably resent their life-situation. They are impatient for new changes. The rural youth are migrating to urban centres in large numbers. Reservation of jobs in government services with eligibility now upto 50 per cent or more for members of lower and middle castes, hardly give them new hope. It rather stares a majority of the youth from among these castes, with mocking irony when they cannot get jobs reserved for them either due to lack of education or simply because the jobs do no exist. On the other hand, the youth coming from sections not qualified for reservation, have a sense of disenchantment of a different nature. They perceive the policy of reservation not only as a gimmick of vote-bank opportunism but also as withdrawal from ideals of establishing a modern liberal society in India with a premium on merit and performance. With government job opportunities narrowing for such youth, we find them increasingly drawn to sectors of professional and economic opportunities outside the control of the state. It is a healthy development because it motivates these youth towards higher levels of performance. It is this section which is seeking maximum level of opportunities offered by a liberalized global economy. Thus, we find the degree of desire for mobility to be equally higher both among the rural youth who yearn to migrate to the cities within the country as also among the middle class urban youth who wish to migrate in search of global opportunities available within the country or abroad. But youth, whether in cities or in villages, share disenchantment from the 'present' in an equal measure.

These factors have long-term and deeper consequences for our society and its direction of social change. At one level, the increasing disenchantment of the youth and their parents is used for mobilization of primordial identities, such as caste, region and religion etc. On the other, the new psychological and motivational forces create values and structures which contain the seeds of transcending primordialities through institutions and associations articulating cosmopolitan interests. It probably results from multiple contradictory effects of forces of media exposure, enhanced levels of cultural and communication contacts with diverse lifestyles and values across regions and nations. Obviously, the emerging technology-culture interface does not recognize primordial or regional social boundaries. Yet, in this process, crystallization also of primordial identities gains strength along with the growth of its opposite, that is consolidation of inter-cultural transactions and globalization of styles of life. We notice this happening in our own country where styles of dress, culinary arts and preferences, rituals and aesthetic practices, which a few decades ago had only a regional existence, have today gained national spread and acceptance.

There is yet another deeper significance of these changes. In the long run, it is bound to erode the life expectations anchored mainly upon primordial loyalties. This may happen first because of the cumulative effect of the inter-cultural exposures and heightened self-consciousness among the younger generation, contributing to autonomy of choice making. The disenchantment from the 'present' which we noted as a common moral attribute of the younger generation in India, irrespective of their class, caste and religious affiliations, is bound to play a contributory role in this process. Its relationship with changing patterns of family, kinship and marriage ties and formations of new individual identities, points to the future direction of social change.

A question arises: how do these changes affect the future of our political culture, organization and participation? Would these forces strengthen or weaken the democratic process of nation-building? What role will politics play in our life as we enter the twenty-first century? The emergent forces of social change offer us some insight into the future scheme of political processes and their form. Firstly, the principles of political legitimacy are bound to be radically altered. With higher levels of education and social mobility and enlargement of social, economic and cultural space for choice making by citizens, the overwhelming and monopolistic role that political institutions and parties have so far played in people's life, is bound to shrink. It is going to affect both the role of the state and the political parties. The legitimacy of political parties based mainly on support from mobilization of primordial identities, such as caste, ethnicity and religion, would face increasing competition from numerous alternate sources and principles of political mobilization and political demands. Accountability of political performance, both at the leadership and party levels, would sharpen with this development. The space that politics occupies in our life today may decline and issues of political legitimacy and accountability may form basic concerns of citizens.

Such changes are emergent in our society and culture today. These will strengthen the democratic process since they redefine the role of politics and political parties in our social life. The pangs of social transformation that we experience today, the debasement of the political culture or its criminalization etc., that we notice give an appearance of invincibility. Looking deeper into the nature and direction of new social forces emerging in society, it is not difficult, however, to recognize their transient nature. There are powerful new social, cultural and motivational impulses competing for a space in our life which enjoy substantial autonomy over forces of primordial identities. The process of systemic mobilization and consolidation of these forces has not only begun but is gaining momentum. It is evident from growth in the emphasis on decentralization, proliferation of non-governmental organizations, voluntary associations, special interest groups, and identities. The new movements for the protection of ecology, human rights, rights of women, children and marginalized groups, etc., are indicators of the new directions of social change.

SOCIOLOGY AND THE CHALLENGE OF CHANGE

The study of social change has been the central concern of Indian sociology. Even when sociologists or social anthropologists studied ethnography of a village, a tribe or a community, an implicit focus on change existed in their frame of reference. With few exceptions, from the 1960s, the study of change began to focus upon public policy, administration and planning process in rural and urban areas. Specializations in sociology multiplied and studies became more analytical and self-conscious of theory and methodology. Still, the major analytical categories were those of caste, class, tribe and communities. Policy-oriented rural and urban surveys were undertaken, the interest being on planned transformation of society. The studies of social movements were added on to these interests of sociologists beginning in the 1970s. It led to a more comprehensive theoretical analysis of change. The focus increasingly shifted from study of change as reflected through structures to that of comprehension of its processes. Social movement studies have a special significance in this respect. These studies also introduced diverse theoretical and methodological orientations in the studies of change. Overarching these shifts in theory and methodology, a debate on the indigenization of categories persisted. The discussions ranged from a quest for 'a sociology for India' to experimental explorations in 'ethno-sociology'.

The question arises as to what new challenges does Indian sociology encounter as it seeks to analyze the emerging new forces of social change? To what extent have its conceptual and methodological elements responded to deal with emergent new realities? One noticeable innovation in this respect can be seen in the study of new social movements. Examples are that of the Dalit movements, gender and eco-feminist movements and human rights movements etc. Like many other trends in Indian sociology, a large part of the theoretical and conceptual apparatus in these studies is global in character. One might mention the departure in these studies from uses of formal concepts like class or caste and their replacement with processual notions, for example, 'exploitation' and 'domination'. It is assumed that on subjects like gender discrimination or denial of human rights to the children, the aged and the minorities, meaningful studies are not those which factorize concerns based on class or caste, but those which observe degrees of exploitation and domination irrespective of such boundaries. No matter whether a woman or an elderly person or a member of the cultural minority belongs to a rich or a poor home, they may be equally susceptible to suffer discrimination and maltreatment across class or caste boundaries. A new perspective on conceptual orientations may, therefore, be required.

Related to this challenge in sociology is the emerging plurality of values defining the paradigms of sociology. Plurality of paradigms has been an intrinsic feature of sociology. There is hardly one single book or single methodology that a sociologist can prescribe to his students representing the paradigm of sociology. Even the works of its pioneers, for example, Karl Marx, Max Weber and Emile Durkheim, contained multiple paradigms as reflected in varying degrees at different stages of their writings. Hence, what is new today is not the debate about the plurality of paradigms, but a seeming emphasis on the fragmentation of the normative basis of sociology. This too is a global process. Yet, it may be useful to discuss its historicity in Indian sociology.

NORMATIVE BASE OF SOCIOLOGY

Let us now examine the normative base of sociology and the tremors that it encounters today. This normative base is essentially characterized by spirit of consensuality. Consensuality offers freedom of choice in human interaction and decision-making and thus, it logically legitimizes dissent. Consensus and dissent constitutes the dialetic of society. In concrete social manifestation, this normative base finds expression in principles of democracy, secularism and human rights. Consequently, the existence of sociology as a discipline is threatened if the legitimacy of these basic institutions and values is threatened. The history of sociology bears ample testimony to this fact.

For this reason, the worldview of sociology accommodates within its framework many sociological traditions that recognize the role of conflict and dissent. It also accommodates universal as well as particularistic concerns. As the pace of social change accelerates, as we see in India today, there is proliferation of myriad particularistic concerns based on caste, religion, ideology and interests etc. These give impetus to growth of alternate sociological formulations and studies, such as sociologies of gender, minorities, ethnic groups, Dalits and other marginalized sections of society. The concerns of sociology may extend to studies of new social movements and problems of ecology and its sustainability in the process of economic development. The role of voluntary associations has increased in most studies in these areas. A large number of sociologists are engaged both as social activists and researchers through these bodies. Their contributions today constitute an alternate or a distinct sociological tradition impinging upon sociology's theory, concepts and methods. In many areas, these studies diverge from those conducted in universities and colleges by academic sociologists. Normative tensions in sociology emerge from this diversity. When social activists with particularistic goals make pronouncements on larger issues of equality, justice and exploitation etc., from their limited perspective, it brings into play the tensions of relationship between universal and particular levels of observation. It leads to not only fragmentation of the normative basis of sociology but also schism in its central discourse. Eventually, there may be a temptation to look at the normative basis of sociology from a sectarian perspective. The challenge that Indian sociology is likely to face today is not merely of the crisis in its central paradigm on the issues of metatheory or its grounding in reality, but also from the danger of delegitimization of the very basis of normative consensuality. The challenges of change in our society exert pressures which necessitate that our profession extends its thinking on concepts and methods, on universal and particularistic levels of sociological discourses to take into account new compulsions which recognize diversity and identity in achieving consensuality.

This can be achieved by our profession, particularly those in the academia, through conscious efforts to establish bridges through dialogue, participation and partnership with activist sociologists may eventually help in evolving a unity of discourse between them. Such interaction through highly desirable exchange of discourse may eventually help in evolving a common discourse between the academic and activist sociologists. Some beginnings have already been made; for example, one may mention gender sociology and the studies of new social movements. There is need to strengthen and enlarge such interests. It would reduce the hiatus that otherwise seemingly develops between the sectarian and consensual foci in the paradigms of sociology.

In addition, as sociologists, we confront challenges which are not merely related to ideological problems of a universal or indigenous paradigm of sociology. One may even say, this problem is now behind us because of substantial growth that our profession has made since independence. A rich tradition of theoretical and methodological criticism has been institutionalized in sociology. The social and cultural changes in society have contributed to a level of maturity and stability in the profession. However, a very substantial reason for this stability and self-assurance is due to rich stock of sociological studies that have been conducted and published by Indian sociologists and institutions of research.

Some professional anxiety, however, still remains. It seems that a massive ideological transition is slowly taking place in our society. There is a manifest pull towards values of achievement and entrepreneurial adventure. With increased global networking of economy, modes of consumption and cultural styles, a new resurgence of aspirations is taking place. It affects the career preferences of people and their perception of the life-world. Globalization and liberalization of economy also creates new opportunities and demands for certain types of skills and education which may pull away an increasing number of scholars and students from liberal and humanistic social sciences such as sociology. It is not that such value preferences did not exist in the past. Now, its scale is going to be very large indeed. Also, the scope and the level of opportunities are going to be substantially enlarged.

Teaching and research in sociology could be affected due to these developments. It will pull us both in positive and negative directions. The positive result may be that a large number of students who come to study sociology not as a matter of choice but due to closure of better opportunities, would move away from studying sociology. A large proportion of our undergraduate and graduate student community belongs to this category. There may be added incentive among students to shorten the time-span between education and productive employment. The new forces of change are likely to give huge impetus to go for vocational education. This change may affect the discipline of sociology. There will be pressure for restructuring of courses, methods of teaching and areas of research.

These concerns may coincide with some negative consequences for sociology. As market forces expand, not only our economic life but also our culture and our valuation of knowledge undergo change. Our choices seek optimization of material rewards. In education, employment opportunities play a major role. Hence, enrolment in humanities, social sciences or even many basic areas of natural sciences decreases. This utilitarian pressure may tempt sociologists to tailor sociology to market forces. The question is how far can we vocationalize sociology or make it market-relevant without distorting its core? In my opinion, sociologists may be well advised to think deeply on this issue. The developed societies which have been living with market forces for some years have evolved a balance. Sociology as a branch of knowledge should enkindle among its students skills to apperceive social reality from a perspective, which is simultaneously humanistic, philosophical and scientific. From a holistic perspective of observation, sociology seeks to comprehend reality with critical concerns. It is, therefore, problem-solving in a broader sense of the term. People may study sociology to solve individual problems, as they have done in some societies. The study of sociology also contributes to skills to critically explore and resolve social problems.

The strength of sociology as a discipline lies in its ability to unravel the mysteries of the surface social phenomena or events in their deeper structural contexts as a whole. In this respect, the sociological reasoning takes into account not only the immediate present, but also the past of a social event. Sociological training, therefore, should not only enable its students to cope up with the market forces but inculcate in its student ability to critically comprehend the place of these forces in the scheme of social order from a critical historical perspective. It is, therefore, necessary to keep this aspect of conceptual and methodological training of sociologists intact. Sociology cannot be taught meaningfully without locating its concepts in the context of a worldview of social order and social change. This worldview inheres normative projects about the meanings of social relationships, social forms and institutions as human products. This perspective constitutes the essence of sociology. These need to be preserved as we come to face the challenge of market forces in the realm of acknowledge. This worldview provides the limit within which pragmatic innovation in sociology teaching could be introduced without hurting its essence.

Index